THE GREATEST MANAGEMENT PRINCIPLE IN THE WORLD

Also by Michael LeBoeuf

WORKING SMART
IMAGINEERING
THE PRODUCTIVITY CHALLENGE

THE GREATEST MANAGEMENT PRINCIPLE IN THE WORLD

Michael LeBoeuf, Ph.D.

G. P. PUTNAM'S SONS   New York

G. P. Putnam's Sons
Publishers Since 1838
200 Madison Avenue
New York, NY 10016

Library of Congress Cataloging in Publication Data

LeBoeuf, Michael.
    The greatest management principle in the world.

    Includes index.
    1. Personnel management.   2. Incentives in industry.
3. Managing your boss.   I. Title.
HF5549.L38   1985   650.1   84-26597
ISBN 0-399-13052-7

Printed in the United States of America
    2   3   4   5   6   7   8   9   10

Acknowledgments

With special thanks to:

Artie and Richard Pine; every author needs a good agent and I have the two best ones in the business.

Adrienne Ingrum for her outstanding editing, encouragement and support. Because of Adrienne I feel like a born-again writer.

My wife, Nancy, whose encouragement and support mean so much to me.

Betty Wishard and Rena Wolner for their constructive suggestions.

Marie Radosti for her excellent typing of the manuscript.

TO RICHARD PINE

A rising star in the publishing world whose persistence and encouragement convinced me that this book must be written.

Contents

PART III: ACTION

Does This Sound Like Where You Work?

Is your company or organization ignoring the greatest management principle in the world (let's call it GMP)? Take this quiz and find out. Check "yes" or "no" to the following twenty questions about your employer, your boss and yourself. If you can't answer a question with a definite yes or no, give the answer that has the balance of weight on its side. A qualified yes is a "yes" and a qualified no is a "no." Work rapidly because the purpose of this exercise is to capture your gut-level impressions about where you work.

Does your employer:

	YES	NO
1. Seem much more interested in short-run payoffs than long-run prosperity?	☐	☐
2. Have lots of people in motion but not much getting done?	☑	☐
3. Discourage risk taking by penalizing those who take unsuccessful chances?	☐	☑
4. Believe that the way the company has always done a job is the only way to do it?	☑	☐

	YES	NO

5. Pay some of the highest salaries at a given level to the recently hired and those who threaten to leave? ☑ ☐

6. Have trouble with political games and backstabbing when it comes to raises, promotions, commissions and perks? ☐ ☑

7. Award the largest budget increases and new staff positions to those who spend the most? ☐ ☑

8. Find it nearly impossible to make rapid decisions or changes because of a morass of policies, procedures, forms and committees? ☐ ☐

9. Talk a lot about the importance of commitment and loyalty to the company but regularly lay off and fire employees? ☐ ☐

10. Have difficulty getting people to work together because everybody's busy looking out for number one? ☐ ☐

Does your boss:

11. Favor those who look busy and dedicated over those who quietly produce results? ☐ ☐

12. Work long hours and/or take home briefcases stuffed with paper? ☐ ☐

13. Expect work of the highest quality and want it by yesterday? ☐ ☐

14. Never remember when you're right and never forget when you're wrong? ☐ ☐

15. Have difficulty understanding why people aren't more committed to their jobs? ☐ ☐

Do you:

	YES	NO
16. Feel like a fool for working hard because there's little or no relationship between how well you do your job and how you are rewarded?	☐	☐
17. Know you could do a better job in less time but don't dare to because you fear being let go or given more work?	☐	☐
18. Have lots of good ideas that could help the organization but don't share them because no one is likely to listen and there's nothing in it for you if they do?	☐	☐
19. Have to complain loudly to get what you want because the squeaking joint gets the grease and those who quietly do their jobs are ignored?	☐	☐
20. Frequently go home exhausted with the feeling that you wasted the day on a lot of useless meetings, paperwork and interruptions?	☐	☐

To find your score, count the number of yes answers.

A SCORE OF:	MEANS:
0–3	Rare and outstanding! Count your blessings. Your organization is practicing GMP. Read on to learn precisely how it works.
4–6	Very good but there's room for improvement, which can be gained by using GMP.
7–9	Significant signs of ignoring GMP.

A SCORE OF:	MEANS:
10–20	Welcome to the club. In the shuffle of daily activities, your outfit has lost sight of GMP.

Introduction

Eureka! After twenty years of reading, consulting with, writing about and working in organizations I have discovered the greatest management principle in the world. It's so simple and obvious that it almost defies description. But it's the one key principle that most of our profit and nonprofit organizations have chosen to ignore. In this short book I will teach you the greatest management principle (GMP) and present a complete program that shows you how to use it to manage people, manage your boss and manage yourself.

Don't be fooled by the size and simplicity of this book. Time is money and you have more important things to do than wade through a verbose treatise on management. You need fast, specific, practical help based on solid research. GMP gives you just that. As you will soon find out, it works!

To get the best results, follow this six-point program:

1. Read the book slowly with a pencil or pen in your hand. Underline key passages and make notes to yourself in the margin. If you think something is particularly important, dog-ear the page or write the page number in the front of the book.

2. Make a photocopy of the summary of GMP on pages

136–37 and put it on the top of your desk or someplace where you will see it frequently every day.

3. For the next week, take a few minutes each day and page through the book, noting the high points you marked. It's much easier to apply a principle when it is totally familiar to you and ingrained in your subconscious. And the key to familiarity is repetition.

4. After several readings, write action plans for managing others, managing your boss and managing yourself, following the steps outlined in the summary.

5. Set deadlines for completing each action plan.

6. Make something happen!

I am not exaggerating when I say that this one simple, but often overlooked, principle is the greatest key to successful management. Although this book focuses on the world of business, GMP is equally applicable to understanding and managing a home, school, family, church, hospital, government agency or any situation in which people work together. No other principle is so universally powerful when it comes to getting things done. Are you ready to make it work for you?

PART I

THE BASICS

The Greatest Management Principle in the World

> *The obscure we eventually see. The completely obvious, it seems, takes longer.*
>
> —EDWARD R. MURROW

When asked if she believed in reincarnation, a personnel chief for the New York City Health Department replied: "Indeed yes. I witness a demonstration every day at five o'clock when dead employees come to life in time to go home."

The message is clear. America's organizations need to get better results—and fast. Inefficiency and waste are running rampant. And foreign competitors are breathing down our backs. We have a choice. We can either find ways to work together more effectively or resign ourselves to living poorer.

Please don't mistake me for a prophet of gloom and doom. I feel very fortunate to live and work in the greatest nation in the history of the world. Our future is exciting and our potential for economic success is unlimited. But to reach those heights we need to make a fundamental change in the way we manage most of our organizations and the people in them. That change is what this book is about.

If you doubt that many of our public and private organizations are having serious problems, consider the facts:

> • In recent years the productivity growth rate of America's companies has been poorer than that of any major industrial nation, including Great Britain. And productiv-

ity growth is the key to increasing the standard of living.

• Every year our schools turn out millions of young people who lack the basic skills necessary for success in an information-oriented economy.

• The quality and value of United States goods in basic industries such as steel, automobiles and electronics have been surpassed by those of foreign nations with efficient, modern industries. As a result, Americans are buying more from abroad than foreign nations are buying from America, and wealth is being drained out of the country.

• No matter how much tax money our government collects, it just can't seem to balance the budget. Consequently, we face huge government deficits that threaten to shake the very foundation of our economy.

• A research study of American workers by Theodore Barry and Associates revealed that white-collar workers spend 50 percent of their time on the job doing nothing! Blue-collar workers, on the other hand, are much more efficient. They're idle only 40 percent of the time.

• Our public and private organizations have the highest number of managers per worker of any nation on earth. Yet when asked to name the leading cause of America's organizational problems, the overwhelming majority of managers answered "poor management."

Enter the Experts

Several years ago, I launched my own study, hoping to find some answers to this widespread management crisis. In an attempt to gain greater insight, I gathered as many different viewpoints as I could get my hands on. I studied management problems, time management and Japanese management. I looked at quality circles and quality of work life. I explored ways to turn the new breed of young workers on to work and to harness the productivity of older ones. I reviewed various methods used to set goals, manage stress, solve problems creatively and cut down paperwork and red tape. I listened to and read the works of some of our most highly regarded scholars, economists, consultants and politicians. One thing became quite clear: If you read and hear enough viewpoints from enough experts, the odds are good you will be totally confused.

Some talked about how complex the problems were, which led me to believe that they were just as confused as I was. As a professor, I learned long ago that if you don't understand what's going on or don't want to commit yourself to a course of action, just talk about the complexity of a problem. It makes you sound knowledgeable and gets you off the hook.

Still others sought to find scapegoats. Some of the more frequently mentioned ones were Wall Street capitalists, greedy unions, lazy workers, foreign competitors, poor managers and, of course, the government. It's only human to blame others when things go wrong. But fixing the blame doesn't fix the problem any more than talking about the complexity of it does.

Others came forth with multitudes of ideas for getting things back on track. Each supported his pet prescription with a rash of economic theories, statistics and assumptions about how the world works. And no two came close to being in agreement. It reminded me of the old poem about six blind men who each felt a different part of an elephant. One felt the side and argued the elephant was like a wall. Another felt a leg and argued the elephant was like a tree. A third grabbed an ear and argued the elephant was like a leaf, and so on. And the poem concluded that the men argued loud and long, though each was partly in the right and all were in the wrong.

The First Clue

All the rhetoric, complexity and confusion left me feeling totally frustrated. I was suffering from a bad case of information overload. But then I remembered the advice one of my professors gave me many years ago:

> *When you can't understand a problem, go back to the basics and you'll start finding some answers. The greatest truths are too important to be new.*

Remembering the professor's words was my first giant step toward discovering GMP. It caused me to look at the problem more objectively and ask myself, "What's basically wrong with most of today's organizations?" The answer was simple:

They need to make better use of their resources and to do a better job of fulfilling their mission. Many aren't doing things right, and some aren't even doing the right things.

But that led to an even more basic question: "Why are they behaving that way?"

The Revelation

At first it seemed like I was right back where I had started. But then I remembered another piece of advice I had learned:

When you have immersed yourself in a problem and are totally perplexed, forget about it and turn your attention to other things. Then, someday when you least expect it, the answer will appear.

At this point, that was one bit of advice I was more than eager to take. I was tired of wrestling with the problem, and "Who knows," I thought, "it might work. It worked for Newton, Darwin and Archimedes. Maybe it will work for me."

And work it did! About six months later the elusive flash of insight I had been looking for appeared. "Good grief! Eureka! That's it! Now, everything makes sense!" It all came together when I heard the parable of the man, the snake and the frog.

A weekend fisherman looked over the side of his boat and saw a snake with a frog in its mouth. Feeling sorry for the frog, he reached down, gently removed the frog from the snake's mouth and let the frog go free. But now he felt sorry for the hungry snake. Having no food, he took out a flask of bourbon and poured a few drops into the snake's mouth. The snake swam away happy, the frog was happy and the man was happy for having performed such good deeds. He thought all was well until a few minutes passed and he heard something knock against the side of his boat and looked down. With stunned disbelief, the fisherman saw the snake was back—with two frogs!

The fable carries two important lessons:

1. You get more of the behavior you reward. You *don't* get what you hope for, ask for, wish for or beg for. *You get what you reward.* Come what may, you can count on people and creatures to do the things that they believe will benefit them most.

2. In trying to do the right things it's oh so easy to fall into the trap of rewarding the wrong activities and ignoring or punishing the right ones. The result is that we hope for A, unwittingly reward B and wonder why we get B.

The following story provides a classic example:

A young machinist asked for three days' vacation to go deer hunting. His supervisor refused the request because the department was very pressed and was being forced to work overtime and on Saturdays. The machinist, who had a record of tardiness, came to work thirty minutes late and the harassed supervisor told him: "If you are tardy one more time this month, you'll be suspended for three days without pay." Guess who was late the next day? The machinist saw the monetary threat as an opportunity and showed up late. He was suspended, went deer hunting and got what he wanted. And management applied the "proper" disciplinary procedure. But the work didn't get done.

By now you probably understand the greatest management principle in the world:

THE THINGS THAT GET REWARDED GET DONE

The greatest single obstacle to the success of today's organizations is the giant mismatch between the behavior we need and the behavior we reward. For example:

• We need top managers to make sound, long-range decisions, but we pay them huge bonuses based on short-term profits and threaten their jobs when profits take a dive. The result? Managers maximize short-term profits, invest less money in people and equipment, and the companies stagnate.

• We need middle managers to conserve costs and minimize red tape, but we reward them with budget increases and new staff assistants when they create more red tape. And conscientious, cost-conserving middle managers who underspend their projected budget get their budgets slashed the following year. The result? Everybody spends all of the budget whether or not it's needed.

• We need white-collar workers who will reduce the huge amounts of needless paperwork. But their job security is directly proportional to the amount of paper they have to shuffle. The result? More paper.

• We need highly productive factory workers, but we don't pay them to produce. Instead, we pay them by the hour, offer them little or no job security and grant pay increases only when they strike, grieve and resort to a host of counterproductive activities. The result? Workers do the minimum amount necessary to keep their jobs, think up restrictive work rules and resist technical changes.

In each case managers and workers behave poorly not because of ignorance, stupidity or laziness. They behave the way the reward system has taught them to behave. Given their circumstances, it's quite likely you and I would do the exact same things.

That great philosopher Yogi Berra once said, "You can observe a lot just by watching." Look around your workplace and you will certainly find examples of the right behavior being ignored or punished and the wrong behavior being rewarded. For example, does your organization:

• Need better results but reward those who look busiest and work the longest hours?
• Ask for quality work but set unreasonable deadlines?
• Want solid solutions to problems but reward quick fixes?
• Talk about company loyalty but offer no job security

and pay the highest salaries to the most recently hired and those who threaten to leave?

• Need simplicity but reward those who complicate matters and generate trivia?

• Ask for a harmonious work environment but reward squeaking joints who complain the most?

• Need creative workers but chastise those who dare to be different?

• Talk about frugality but award the largest budget increases to those who exhaust all of their resources?

• Ask for teamwork but reward one team member at the expense of another?

• Need innovation but penalize unsuccessful risks and reward going by the book?

You probably answered yes to at least several of those questions because those are ten of the most frequent mistakes in rewarding people on the job.

On the other hand, establishing the proper link between performance and rewards is the single greatest key to improving organizations. When we think of the success of a business, most of us think in terms of dollars, cents, statistics, facts and figures. But all the data and charts are nothing more than mere symbols that represent the collective *behavior* of human beings. Reward people for the right behavior and you get the right results. Fail to reward the right behavior and you will likely get the wrong results. That's the simple message of GMP . . . but is it actually so simple?

The Magic Question

> *As I grow older I pay less attention to what men say. I just watch what they do.*

—ANDREW CARNEGIE

The Sister stood before her very young parochial-school class. She held up a shiny silver dollar and said, "I'll give this dollar to the first boy or girl who can name the greatest man who ever lived."

"Was it Michelangelo?" asked a little Italian boy.

"No," replied the Sister. "Michelangelo was a brilliant artist but he wasn't the greatest man who ever lived."

"Was it Aristotle?" asked a little Greek girl.

"No," the Sister answered. "Aristotle was a great thinker and the father of logic, but he wasn't the greatest man who ever lived."

Finally, after several more incorrect answers, a little Jewish boy raised his hand and said, "I know who it was, Sister. It was Jesus Christ."

"That's right," she replied and promptly gave him the dollar.

Being somewhat surprised at the Jewish boy's answer, she approached him on the playground at recess and asked, "Nathan, do you really believe Jesus Christ was the greatest man who ever lived?"

"Of course not, Sister," Nathan replied. "Everybody knows Moses was the greatest. But business is business."

You don't need a doctorate in psychology to understand why Nathan behaved the way he did. All you have to do is ask the magic question:

| *"WHAT'S BEING REWARDED?"* |

Managers, workers, teachers, students, doctors, politicians, all of us behave the way the reward system teaches us to behave. Nathan understood the reward system and, like any normal person, chose to make it work for him.

In recent years pollsters have been finding two seemingly conflicting answers to two very important questions about work:

1. Are Americans holding back effort from their jobs and giving less than they are capable of giving?
Answer. Definitely yes.
2. Is the American work ethic dying, or has it deteriorated in recent years?
Answer. Definitely no.

If American workers deeply believe in the value and importance of hard work, why aren't they willing to give it? Ask the magic question—"What's being rewarded?"—and you'll find the answer.

People withhold their best efforts when they see little or no relationship between what they do and how they are rewarded. And that's a common problem for over 75 percent of the American labor force. As one middle manager put it:

> I learned a few years ago that the difference between busting my gut and taking it easy is about $2000 a year before taxes. So now, instead of aiming for the maximum possible, I shoot for the minimum acceptable.

Withholding effort is a big enough problem all by itself. But that's just the tip of the iceberg. When you compare the behavior that is needed with the behavior that is rewarded, one fact comes through loud and clear: Many of our organizations and institutions are covered with negative incentives. Simply put, there are all sorts of inducements and rewards for counterproductive behavior. To illustrate, let's look at three common work situations.

1. On the factory floor.
2. In the white-collar bureaucracy.
3. In the executive suite.

The Factory-Floor Syndrome

In the past several years American executives have journeyed to Japan in droves. They marvel at the motivation, enthusiasm and dedication of Japanese factory workers and ask, "Why aren't our guys like that?" The answer becomes obvious when you compare the ways Japanese and American factory workers are rewarded.

The typical Japanese factory worker in a large company has a lifetime-guaranteed job and about 40 percent of his annual income is determined by company productivity and profitability. If the company does well, he shares the prosperity. If the company does poorly, his income is less but he isn't furloughed or fired. And a new robot or computer doesn't threaten his livelihood. If automation replaces his old job, he knows he will be retrained, assigned a new job and still be allowed to share in the profits. Therefore he is eager to accept and find new ways to make the factory more productive because it stands to make him richer. In short, Japanese factories get high productivity because they reward high productivity.

On the other hand, most American factories operate with a very different reward system. First, there is little or no job security, and factory workers are usually the first to be furloughed during hard times. Second, most workers aren't paid on the basis of what is produced and sold; they are paid by the hour. And do they get rewarded for being more productive? Not usually. And, as I mentioned before, most factory workers have to grieve, strike, threaten, complain and resort to a host of counterproductive activities to get a wage or benefit increase.

Because the American factory worker lacks job security, he sees new technology as a threat rather than an asset to his livelihood. A new computer or robot is likely to replace him or one of his colleagues on the assembly line. And he is never going to think up a new labor-saving way to do the job. That could be economic suicide! His incentives are to produce the minimum amount to keep his job, create restrictive work rules, demand greater benefits and resist technological changes. Who can blame him? The reward system has encouraged him to do so.

Needless to say, the Japanese reward system has a very healthy payoff. For example, it takes about two hundred man hours for United Automobile Workers members to manufacture and assemble parts to create an American car. Japanese workers take one hundred hours to do the job—and some would argue that they do it better. In socialist Sweden, managers who plan production have to allow for about 20 percent employee absenteeism. In Japan, they don't even have a word for it.

White-Collar Wheel Spinning

Factory-floor problems are bad enough, but there is a much bigger enemy lurking in the offices where most of us work. That enemy is bureaucracy. The enormous growth of top-heavy bureaucracies in our profit and nonprofit organizations is a gigantic obstacle to productivity. It's bureaucracy that forces today's nurses to spend half their time filling out forms instead of caring for patients. It's bureaucracy that requires teachers to spend untold hours writing reports and attending conferences instead of preparing lessons, grading papers and counseling students. It's bureaucracy that prevents young executives from becoming leaders by turning them into paper shufflers instead of people developers.

Stop for a moment and think about where you work. Have new layers of management been added in the past decade? Is the volume of internally generated paperwork and reports increasing? Has the number of secretarial and administrative assistants increased in the past decade? Are you spending more time at meetings and doing more paperwork than ever? We are rapidly becoming a nation of people who spend a lot of time and energy creating red tape for each other instead of doing productive work. Why? Ask the magic question. "What's being rewarded?"

We have so much unnecessary red tape because we reward those who create it. On a factory floor it's easy to measure productivity and spot wasted effort. But unfortunately, the tools of work measurement haven't been transferred from the factory floors to most of our offices. Consequently, the temptation to confuse activity with productivity and to reward activities regardless of their value is overwhelming.

Those who work the longest hours, write the longest reports and serve on the most committees are much more visible and more likely to be rewarded than those who ask, "Why do it if it isn't necessary?" The middle manager who exhausts the budget, attends endless meetings and generates reams of reports and memoranda is often rewarded with a promotion, budget increase and even an administrative assistant to help him cope with his massive workload. On the other hand, the middle manager who quietly conserves costs, does his job and holds trivia to a minimum is likely to be regarded as less dynamic and less committed.

Once an organization starts rewarding busy behavior, it's sure to get more of the same. And the accumulated red tape snowballs into activities that become ends in themselves. Meetings become weekly meetings, reports become monthly reports, printouts become daily printouts and committees become standing committees. Precious time and energy that could be used to get positive results are poured into needless activities that few will ever question. Everybody complains about all the red tape and how overworked they are, but the red tape will exist and continue to grow as long as there are rewards for it.

The Executive's Enigma

Sony Chairman Akio Morita summed it up best: "American managers are too concerned about short-term profits and too little concerned about their workers." In recent years we have come to realize that top managers, the people to whom we entrust the long-term welfare of our companies, are enormously preoccupied with maximizing short-term profits. "What's wrong with that?" you ask. "Isn't the purpose of a business to make a profit?"

The problem is that the price a company pays for short-term profit maximization can be long-term stagnation. Every dollar a company declares as profit and pays out to stockholders is a dollar that won't be invested in basic research, new plants and equipment, and training and updating of employee skills. It's much like the farmer who sells all of this year's corn crop at the market and has none to plant the following season. Or a sixteen-year-old who quits school because he is bored and can get a low-paying job that looks like big bucks to him.

And the results of short-sighted executive thinking are taking a huge toll. For example, Japanese assembly lines are much more automated than ours. In recent years, the average age of American plants and equipment has been almost double that of Japan's. Some of our steel mills are still using turn-of-the-century technology, while the Japanese retool every ten years. As David Roderick, chairman of U.S. Steel, put it, "You can't win a race if your opponent is in a Mercedes SL and you put your guy in a Model T Ford." Why is top management so short-sighted? Ask the magic question: "What's being rewarded?"

The pressure starts on Wall Street, where corporations raise capital by selling stock. And the best-selling stocks are those that have the fastest payoffs with the least risk. You don't sell the future on Wall Street. You sell the present. And you sell the present by looking very profitable now. Consequently, companies provide very large rewards to top-level executives for short-term profits. It's possible for a high-level executive to double his total compensation based on current profits. And a CEO who sacrifices short-term profits in the name of long-term investment may find himself looking for another job.

Pretend for a moment that *you* are a high-level executive. You know the company needs to update plant and equipment, retrain workers and invest more in basic research. But if you put the money in short-term profits, there's a fat bonus waiting for you. Sure, you can invest more in the long run, but it probably won't affect you because you will be promoted, retired or working for another company by then. And failing to show a good profit could put you out pounding the pavement and end what has been a successful executive career. What would you do? Only a saint is going to risk his career and forgo such rewards in the name of long-run company prosperity. And there aren't very many saints.

But If You Think Business Has Problems . . .

Needs and rewards aren't only out of sync in the business world, they are also woefully mismatched in the nonprofit and service sectors of society. Here, in brief, are several major problems you can better understand simply by asking the magic question.

HEALTH-CARE COSTS

Have you priced a stay in the hospital lately? It's enough to make you sick. We need the best possible health care at reasonable, affordable cost. But we reward the maximum amount of health care at the highest cost. The overwhelming majority of hospital bills are paid by the government and insurance companies, so the patient doesn't care about costs. All he wants is first-class treatment. And the doctors, clinics and hospitals are more than happy to give it to him because they get paid for whatever they do, whether or not the treatment benefits the patient. Consequently, it is estimated that as much as 30 percent of all treatment is unnecessary. In short, we have written the health-care industry a blank check and they are cashing it. As hospital consultant Donald Beck put it, "If you had fallen asleep in 1960 and dreamed up the most countereffective system of hospital reimbursement, it couldn't match the crazy system that has evolved in real life."

THE DEFICIT

Our leaders can't run the government on the countless billions we pay in taxes every year. Every four years presidential candidates promise to balance the budget. Senators and representatives talk endlessly about how deficits must be eliminated. And the deficits just keep on growing. Why? Ask the magic question.

In this case, the reward is to be elected, and politicians get elected and reelected by making promises and delivering favors to voters. But the government doesn't "produce" anything to give. It can only serve us using what it takes from us in taxes, minus a very large handling fee to run an enormous bureaucracy.

There is no mystery to balancing a budget. You raise taxes and/or cut government spending, but those are very distasteful options that could cost a politician his job. On the other hand, borrowing (or printing) money to pay for government spending doesn't have immediate voter impact. No one has ever lost an election because of the deficit. Until someone does, it's quite likely that the dark clouds of government borrowing and the subsequent high interest rates will plague our economy.

CRIME

The government deficit isn't the only place where an erroneous reward system permeates our society. Why do we have so much crime in America? Ask the magic question.

Look at burglary as a business. Today, less than one out of seven burglaries results in an arrest. Couple this fact with legal delays, backlogged courts and overcrowded prisons and it's possible for even the dumb burglar who gets caught to get off with a minimal sentence or none at all. As Georgia Supreme Court Justice Charles L. Weltner put it, "Right now a person who has been through the system and is contemplating a crime probably views things as follows: (1) If I do it I won't get caught; (2) If I get caught I won't get prosecuted; (3) If I get prosecuted I won't get convicted; (4) If I get convicted I won't go to prison; (5) If I go to prison it won't be for very long." When you consider that nine out of ten new small businesses employing twenty or fewer persons fail in the first year, burglary is an excellent option for an amoral entrepreneur, given the reward system of criminal justice in America.

EDUCATION

Perhaps the greatest crime of all is being committed unwittingly against our children. America's public schools, despite tremendous increases in government spending, have produced approximately 26 million functionally illiterate Americans and another 46 million who are marginally literate.

Two important factors are low teacher salaries and the way teachers are rewarded. As a salesman's output is goods or services sold, a teacher's output is what students learn. But teachers aren't rewarded on the basis of student performance. Instead, they are paid a low, flat wage based on academic degrees, seniority and other arbitrary benchmarks. And they get pay increases by joining a union and resorting to counterproductive activities much like factory workers do. The self-serving bureaucracies of the education system also demand that teachers devote less time to teaching and more time to red tape. Is it any wonder that many of our best teachers have left the classroom for greener pastures? They asked the magic question.

POVERTY AND UNEMPLOYMENT

Poverty, like government spending, crime, education *and business,* involves a reward system. In Florida, a laid-off, $16,000-a-year worker with a wife and two children can get unemployment and public assistance benefits that equal his prior take-home pay. And a $12,000-a-year worker may find his income increases 19 percent as a result of losing his job. In New York state a family of four eligible for a basic welfare grant, shelter allowance, food stamps and Medicaid has an "earned income equivalent" that is 45.4 percent above the minimum wage.

In addition to paying some people to be poor, we hire and pay other people to give money to the poor. That's the poverty industry—government bureaucracies that are rewarded for spending all of this year's budget so they can ask for even more next year. As in defense, education and all government-funded programs, there are few incentives to save and every incentive to spend.

The net result is that each year more of our wealth is transferred from the private sector to the public sector, where there is no bottom line and where inefficiency is rewarded. Before going too far we should remember what Winston Churchill once remarked: "There are two places where socialism will work: In Heaven where it isn't needed; and in Hell where they already have it."

Summary

Take a hard look at our organizations and ask the magic question. It's easy to see why the best-laid plans go astray. No, the problem isn't complex; it's very simple. And it isn't due to lazy workers, government bureaucrats, foreign competitors, greedy unions or incompetent managers. It's that our reward systems are out of whack and are badly in need of improvement. Like the fisherman, we sometimes reward the wrong things and, like the snake, we get rewarded for the wrong things.

A final word of caution is in order. No matter what the reward system is, a small percentage of people will perform brilliantly and a small percentage will perform poorly. A person's performance is governed by other factors as well, such as personal ability, needs, values and off-the-job rewards. But these are factors over which a manager or organization has little or no control. On the other hand, the reward system is the one key factor that can be controlled and most people will respond to it very positively.

The next time you have trouble understanding why people behave the way they do, just ask the magic question and things will come quickly into focus. And when you are ready to get better results by using GMP, ask the second magic question: *"What needs to be rewarded?"*

Part II gives you ten important answers to that one.

PART II

STRATEGY

Now that you understand GMP, the first step toward making it work for you is to know what to reward and what not to reward. Here you will learn ten important kinds of behavior that every manager needs to reward and the ten opposite and undesirable types of behavior that most companies tend to reward.

Reward Solid Solutions Instead of Quick Fixes

Be careful that victories do not carry the seeds of future defeats.

—*BITS & PIECES* MAGAZINE

What would you say if I told you that a company sacrificed its long-term, competitive advantage so that one of its divisions could reach its profit goals for just one quarter? Well, it happened in the case of Bob, a division manager for a manufacturing firm.

As Bob looked over his fourth-quarter profit projections in early December, his first reaction was, "Where's the Maalox?" An economic downturn coupled with new competition had severely reduced sales. Earlier in the day Bob's boss had told him that top management was looking to cut and streamline the administrative ranks early next year. As Bob sat pondering the budget, he kept hearing the boss's words of warning: "Bob, you better make those profit projections or you'll never survive the cuts." Bob, like many managers today, was being pressured to produce a quick fix.

And produce a quick fix he did. Bob laid off 30 percent of his labor force before Christmas, which drastically reduced operating costs and enabled his division to exceed fourth-quarter profit projections by a handsome margin. This pleased the top brass, who had promised great things to stockholders and the financial community. Top management recognized Bob as a corporate hero, winner, moneymaker and gave him a big bonus as a reward for snatching profits from the jaws of red ink. But the story does not end here.

Unfortunately, Bob's quick fix had devastating long-range consequences. For years Bob's company had the luxury of being the only nonunion outfit in the industry. This gave it a tremendous strategic advantage over the competition because it wasn't saddled with the high costs, inflexibility and administrative hassles of restrictive work rules, regulated hiring and promotion policies, wildcat strikes, collective bargaining and so forth. But shortly after the Christmas layoffs, angry workers held a representation election and by summer the entire company (not just Bob's division) was unionized. Incredible as it seems, the company had rewarded Bob for trading a basic strategic advantage for a divisional quarterly profit.

Oren Arnold once described the prayer of the modern American as "Dear God, I pray for patience. And I want it right now!" We live in an "instant" culture that prides itself on having an easy, quick fix for everything. And not surprisingly, this is reflected in our work. Too often we reward each other for short-term, patchwork solutions that ultimately create more problems than they solve.

We all know that in business and in life in general the future belongs to those who prepare for it. But our instant culture has lulled us into believing that tomorrow will always take care of itself. As one frustrated father put it:

> I tried to convince my ten-year-old son to save part of his allowance by telling him the fable about the ant and the grasshopper. I told him how the ant worked and harvested during the summer while the grasshopper played. And how when winter came the grasshopper was left without food or shelter while the ant was warm and secure. Then when I asked him, "What's the lesson to be learned," he replied, "Have a good time until things get tough. Then get yourself a rich old aunt!"

Solid solutions require time, foresight, patience, sacrifice and discipline, but they have large long-run payoffs. The basic difference between solid solutions and quick fixes is the difference between investing in the future and mortgaging it. Which does your company tend to reward? Here are ten examples of each.

Choose the behavior in each column that sounds most like where you work.

A SOLID SOLUTION IS:	A QUICK FIX IS:
1. Making a commitment to a long-range plan and staying with it.	1. Achieving short-run goals at any cost.
2. Regularly retooling and investing in new and better ways to get things done.	2. Using old equipment until it falls apart because that's the cheapest way to go.
3. Treating employees the way you would like to be treated. Investing in the growth and development of an ongoing, committed, well-trained team.	3. Hiring and firing employees as needed.
4. Committing to the development of new and better products and services because innovation is any business's greatest capital asset.	4. Avoiding the development of new products and services unless the payoff is high and the risk is low.
5. Having customer service that generates repeat business.	5. Trying to make a bundle on one quick sale.
6. Maintaining fair and stable prices that generate customer trust and loyalty.	6. Raising and lowering prices to reach current profit goals.
7. Acquiring only those businesses the company has the skills to manage.	7. Venturing into a new industry because the financial gurus promise fast payoff with low risk.
8. Rewarding people, through an ongoing program, for finding ways to work more efficiently.	8. Slashing expenses to the bone in a cost-cutting drive.
9. Emphasizing quality as the key to improving productivity.	9. Delivering the goods on time at any cost.
10. Realizing that the people closest to the job usually know most about it and tapping their brain power.	10. Letting managers make all the decisions because it is faster and they are paid to do so.

To encourage solid solutions and discourage quick fixes, a company or manager can do a number of things.

☐ 1. *Evaluate people over longer time periods.* In addition to yearly evaluations, give each employee a five-year review that looks at his performance over the entire period and give large rewards to the best performers.

☐ 2. *Give long-run rewards.* For example, part of a top manager's yearly bonus might be in stock credits that he can cash in only at retirement or when he leaves the company. That way, his short-run performance will have long-run impact on his own bank account.

☐ 3. *Identify the one or two key factors that are most important to the long-range success of your team and reward people for contributing to those factors.* If quality improvement is most important, reward those who provide the greatest improvements in quality. If teamwork is essential, reward those who help develop cohesion and build morale. If you are after a larger market share, reward those who expand the company's markets. And be sure to tell *everyone* early on what those one or two strategic factors are.

☐ 4. *Give bonuses and recognition to those who make smart, long-run decisions* instead of to those who just look good today.

☐ 5. *Evaluate capital investment decisions in basic research, new products and new plant and equipment over longer time periods* instead of tying them into the quarterly budget.

☐ 6. Like the Japanese, *make a substantial part of every employee's total compensation dependent on company prosperity.* This gives everyone incentive to be productive.

Of course, you can't ignore the short run. Every manager's job includes finding the right trade-off between today's profits and tomorrow's growth. Both are essential. But solid solutions need more attention and greater rewards because they are so much harder to come by. Long-run success in business—or anything—is rare because it is difficult. But as Justice Louis Brandeis advised his impatient daughter, "My dear, if you would only realize that life is hard, things would be so much easier for you."

Are you managing as if tomorrow mattered? Reward solid solutions. They're indispensable. And be wary of quick fixes. Those who dwell on the tricks of the trade never learn the trade.

Reward Risk Taking Instead of Risk Avoiding

Take a chance! All of life is a chance. The man who goes furthest is generally the one who is willing to do and dare. The "sure thing" boat never gets far from shore.

—DALE CARNEGIE

"Why can't I get anybody to take responsibility for anything?" screamed Ed, vice-president of branch administration for a large, multibranch bank. As I walked into Ed's office, it was apparent that he was angry and was having a hard time getting his branch managers to behave like managers.

"I just don't understand it," Ed continued. "I hire these people, expect them to take charge, and all I get is a bunch of damned excuses about why things don't get done. It's gotten so ridiculous that I've started keeping a list. Just look at the excuses I've written down since the beginning of the month." In disgust he threw a tablet on the desk for me to read.

I was too busy.
That's not my branch.
You didn't give me the go-ahead.
That's his job.
I'm not paid to do that.
I forgot.
I didn't think it was important.
I thought you knew that.
My predecessor did it.
I didn't receive the paperwork.
You didn't tell me this was different.

I remembered that one of my former students was working for Ed as a branch manager. "How's young Jack White working out?" I asked.

"White?" he replied. "I believe he's doing a fine job. Let me check."

Ed pulled out a file and started thumbing through it. "Let's see, White's at the Bayview branch. . . . There it is." He paused for a moment to look at the data and then continued.

"Overall, he seems to be doing a fine job. The branch has the lowest number of loan losses. His credit checks are thorough. Teller out of balances are low, but so are the cross-sales ratios of his customer-service representatives. Jack's a hard worker who pays close attention to detail and is very loyal to the bank. You know he started with us as a part-time teller and worked his way up by not making mistakes."

At that point I had heard all I needed to know about Ed's problem.

Have you ever worked for an organization where the rule for getting ahead is "Don't do anything wrong"? It's very unhealthy but terribly common. Good organizations encourage people to take smart risks, give them leeway to be wrong and realize that intelligent mistakes are part of the price you pay for personal and company growth. This healthy approach to managing was best summed up by Stephen Jobs, co-founder of the brilliantly successful Apple Computer, Inc., when he was asked, "How does Apple do it?" Jobs replied, "Well, we hire really great people and we create an environment where people can make mistakes and grow."

We all have a tendency to avoid risks. Let's face it. Failure hurts! Every time you try something new you run the risk of failing. But, ironically, risk avoidance carries the worst risk any person or organization can take. It is the surest guarantee of boredom, frustration, stagnation and ultimate failure.

Not surprisingly, when personality tests are given to low-, average- and top-performing managers, top performers show the greatest tendency to take risks. Low-level performers long for security and try to appear important without taking risks. Average performers are less security-conscious but, like low performers, are preoccupied with looking effective rather than being effective. But peak performers show very different behavior patterns. They tend to enjoy work for its own sake and care less about security. Their strongest desires are for achievement (setting goals and reaching them) and self-actualization (being the best they can). You may want to keep those points in mind the next time you're hiring.

The way to convert risk avoiders into risk takers is to create a climate that promotes, rewards and supports risk taking and gives people the opportunity to learn from their mistakes without fearing repercussions. With that goal in mind, here are several key guidelines to establishing a healthy risk-taking climate:

□ 1. *Teach people that intelligent errors are part of the cost of progress.* A mistake only proves that someone stopped talking long enough to do something! Whenever you try to take great leaps forward, expect to take a few steps back. What's important is to learn from our miscues and keep trying to improve.

□ 2. *Use yourself as an example.* Talk openly and honestly about errors you have made and how you profited and learned from them. Talk about risks you were afraid to take but did take and how taking them made your life better. Point out that you make lots of mistakes and give a recent example or two. (If you aren't making any mistakes, perhaps you aren't trying anything new.)

□ 3. *Don't let yourself or others waste time on small risks.* People who achieve great results tackle great projects. And when you try to do big things, you are going to make big mistakes. So be it. Remember, if Christopher Columbus had turned back, no one would have blamed him. But no one would have remembered him either.

□ 4. *Celebrate both successes and setbacks.* Obviously the greatest rewards and accolades will go to those who take large, successful risks. But, as the old sports axiom goes, winning takes care of itself. We need support and encouragement most when we take a chance, give it our all and fall flat on our face.

The research division of Ore-Ida frozen foods encourages learning and risk taking by shooting off a cannon in celebration every time the "perfect failure" occurs. Management realizes that research is a risky business fraught with failure, and to end up with a few good ideas means starting out with lots of ideas. When a project is not working, rather than let it drag on they shoot off a cannon, have a few good laughs and try another idea. This helps create a positive climate in which employees can keep trying, learning and growing.

☐ 5. *Don't take risks for others or bail them out if things go sour,* or else you deprive them of the chance to learn and grow from experience. Worse, you will probably cause ill feelings and may even be expected to bail them out again! Don't be a rescuer unless you want to become a victim.

☐ 6. *Encourage smart risks, not foolish chances.* The whole purpose of risk taking is to create better people and organizations, not foolhardy daredevils. Smart risks require several key ingredients:

- Have a goal. A risk without a clear purpose is dumb.
- Consider the worst possible outcome and be sure you can live with it.
- Weigh the potential problems and losses against the potential gains. A smart risk is worth it. Have an alternate plan to save yourself if things turn sour.
- Once you decide to take a risk, do your best, call it a success and don't look back. The only real failure is in never risking.
- Limit your losses. If things don't go well, get out before you lose too much. As one sage put it, "If you're losing a tug-of-war with a tiger, give him the rope before he gets to your arm. You can always get another rope."
- Relax, enjoy and learn from your risks. If we didn't take ourselves so seriously, risk avoidance wouldn't be such a big problem. A successful career takes fun and guts. Help yourself to a healthy serving of both.

Establishing a healthy risk-taking climate also sets the stage for the development of every company's greatest capital asset— the subject of the next strategy.

Reward Applied Creativity Instead of Mindless Conformity

Somehow every organization must make room for inner-directed, obstreperous, creative people, sworn enemies of routine and the status quo, always ready to upset the apple cart by thinking up new and better ways of doing things.

—ADMIRAL HYMAN G. RICKOVER

John Andrew Holmes advised, "Never tell a young man that anything can't be done. God may have been waiting for centuries for somebody ignorant enough of the impossible to do that very thing." That's excellent advice, but history is filled with stories of creative people who were told to take their crazy ideas and beat it.

- An irate banker once told an inventor to remove "that toy" from his office. That toy was the telephone.
- A Hollywood producer wrote a curt rejection note on a manuscript. That manuscript became *Gone With the Wind*.
- In 1976 a young engineer got bored with laying out computer chips. On three different occasions he asked if he could work on designing a personal computer but his company said no each time. So he went home, built one and named it the Apple. Today that engineer is worth over a half-billion dollars.
- Many years ago a young clerk working in a hardware store suggested to his boss that he set up a table in the middle of the store and sell off obsolete inventory items for a dime each. The boss agreed, the sale was a big success and this gave the clerk another idea. Why not open a store

that sold only nickel and dime items? He could run the store and the boss could supply the capital. "The plan will never work because you can't find enough items to sell at a nickel or dime," said the boss. The young man was disappointed but decided to try the idea on his own. His former boss later lamented, "As near as I can figure it, every word I used in turning down Woolworth has cost me about a million dollars."

The most important capital asset in any business isn't money, buildings or equipment, but ideas. Einstein believed imagination was more important than knowledge. Shakespeare said that imagination makes man the paragon of animals. And former Quaker Oats president Ken Mason remarked, "I'm not impressed with the power of a corporate president. I am impressed with the power of ideas."

Anybody can come up with new ideas. If you doubt that, consider all the ways we think up to get out of working! Or gather a few people to brainstorm solutions to a problem, and you will discover there are creative people all around you.

What *is* in short supply are innovative people—bullheaded, persistent, never-say-die mavericks who believe so strongly in an idea that they will do whatever it takes to see that idea turned into a working reality. A classic example comes from 3M. Many years ago a young worker kept trying to come up with new uses for rejected sandpaper materials. Management thought he was wasting too much time and fired him. But he continued to go to work! His creative persistence eventually got 3M into the business of making roofing granules for asphalt shingles, and some years later the worker retired from the company as vice-president of the Roofing Granules Division. Today, 3M is one of America's most innovative corporations because it learned from its past and lives by its "eleventh commandment": "Thou shalt not kill a new product idea."

Being for innovation is like being for motherhood. Who could be against it? Yet most organizations just pay lip service to creativity and innovation. They ask for new ideas and then quickly reject them. And when a new idea is accepted, the worker rarely gets a reward proportional to the idea's worth.

The greatest rewards typically go to those with the proper credentials, who follow the right procedures, dress in the proper attire and display the proper attitudes.

No organization can be effective without a reasonable amount of conformity. But innovation also responds to GMP— you get it by asking for it and then rewarding it. Create a climate that encourages new ideas and make innovation part of everyone's job. With that in mind, here are several major ingredients needed to establish an innovative climate:

☐ 1. *Tolerate failure.* Innovation is a numbers game with lots of strikeouts and a few home runs. Most ideas don't become innovations and most innovations are not successful. Persistence and the ability to deal with disappointment, failure and rejection are essential. Keep trying. Point out that winners lose more than losers lose because winners never stop trying. It took Thomas Edison over six thousand tries before he came up with a workable filament for the incandescent lamp. But that one success offset the cost of all those failures a billionfold.

☐ 2. *Create a relaxed, informal work environment* that deemphasizes rules and encourages both solitude and plenty of informal communication. While it's true that every new idea is the product of a single brain, it's also true that people tend to come up with more and better ideas while in groups. Creativity works best in a relaxed, positive atmosphere where people feel accepted and free to be themselves. A few comedians in the group can help create that atmosphere. But be sure that people can also find quiet and solitude when they need to think things through.

☐ 3. *Pay royalties for successful innovations.* This is where most companies really miss the boat, particularly in research and development. In most large American companies workers are forced to sign agreements that give the patent rights for their innovations to the company. And when a successful innovation is born, the employee gets a plaque, a pat on the back or a few hundred dollars, while the top brass celebrate by rewarding themselves with huge bonuses taken from the profits brought in by the innovation. If you were the innovator, what would that do to your motivation? To keep people innovative, give them a piece of the profits. Video game manufacturers, for example, pay their designers royalties of 10 to 15 percent of the profits made on their games. And I can assure you that if the publisher of this book was paying me a flat fee instead of a royalty, I wouldn't be working as hard to write the best book I can. As a new idea makes or saves money, give part of it back to the contributor. It works!

☐ 4. *Encourage competition.* Laboratory research and practical business experience have reached the same conclusion: competition increases innovation. Psychological experiments have shown that competition can increase mental output by 50 percent or more. Internal competition between groups is a great way to encourage innovation. IBM, for example, puts several groups to work on the same problem (such as designing new hardware or software) and conducts "shootouts" to see which group comes up with the best solutions. The spirit and challenge of competition keep people excited and encourage new ideas.

☐ 5. *Support the fanatic.* Peter Drucker wrote, "Whenever anything is accomplished, it is being done, I have learned, by a monomaniac with a mission." Behind any major innovation is an individual consumed by a driving force to make an idea or dream succeed. These are the people who take aim at a target and will the arrow into the bull's eye. The 3M worker who kept going to work after being fired is a case in point.

Fanatics usually don't fit well into the organizational mold. They can be egotistical, obnoxious, impatient, intolerant, distracting and extremely difficult to work with—and those are just their good points! But they are indispensable to successful innovation, and smart managers don't run them off. Instead, they feed their egos by celebrating and rewarding successes and nursing them through trying times and failures.

☐ 6. *Ask everyone to set at least one innovative goal and a deadline for achieving it.* Have everyone write down the answer to this question: "What would you like to do that you aren't doing now that would benefit both you and the company?" Innovation is everybody's business, and the people closest to the job usually come up with the best new ideas for improving their jobs. Tap into that huge reservoir of brain power waiting to be harnessed, and be sure to insist on deadlines. Innovation is like golf—the follow-through counts.

☐ 7. *Teach everyone the basics of creative thinking.* Like any human skill, idea production can be increased and improved with practice and the application of a few simple techniques, like these*:

• Question the status quo and challenge assumptions. When asked what advice he would most like to give to science students, Albert Einstein replied, "I would ask them to spend an hour every day rejecting the ideas of others and thinking out things for themselves. This will be a hard thing to do, but it will be very rewarding." Creative people are never satisfied and are always looking for a better way.

• Look for patterns and similarities in other ideas that can be applied to the problem you are working on. For example, the telephone was conceived by modeling it after the human ear, the camera was modeled after the eye, and the roll-on deodorant applicator was modeled after the ball-point pen.

• Use a different frame of reference. Creativity is making new things seem familiar and familiar things seem new. Woodrow Wilson said it best: "Originality is a fresh pair of eyes." Is a hen only an egg's way of making another egg, as Samuel Butler stated? Is man merely a creature who was made at the end of the week's work when God was tired, as Mark Twain told us? These are examples of fresh perspectives.

• Realize that all new ideas are simply new combinations of old ones. Clarence Birdseye went to Canada and ate some fish that had been frozen and thawed naturally. This gave him the idea for the frozen-foods industry. Ben Franklin got tired of changing eyeglasses. So he combined them and made bifocals. Create an idea bank of clippings, photos, quotations, ads, etc., and pretty soon you will be combining and rearranging them to form ideas of your own.

*Adapted from *Imagineering* by Michael LeBoeuf (McGraw-Hill Book Company, 1980).

• Pay close attention to your hunches. A hunch often comes out of facts stored at the subconscious level. Ask yourself, "Is it possible that I have gained information about this problem without realizing it?" If so, your hunch is probably a good one. Creativity and good hunches go hand in hand.

• Be alert for serendipity (the knack of making accidental, valuable discoveries). Innovation is a companion to unexpected findings. For example, a chemist accidentally broke a bottle containing a liquid plastic substance. When he picked up the pieces of glass, he noticed they stuck together. This accidental discovery led to the development of shatterproof glass.

• Never try to think up ideas and judge them at the same time. It is like trying to step on the brake and the accelerator of your car simultaneously. Think up now, judge later. The best ideas can be destroyed prematurely. Go for quantity.

Years ago one of Ripley's famous *Believe-It-or-Not* cartoons pictured a plain bar of iron worth $5 and pointed out that if you forged the iron into horseshoes, it would then be worth $10.50. If you used the iron for making needles, it would be worth $3,285. And if you turned the iron into watch springs, the value would soar to $250,000. There's a big difference between $5 and $250,000. The difference is applied creativity.

Reward Decisive Action Instead of Paralysis by Analysis

If Moses had been a committee, the Israelites would still be in Egypt.

—ANONYMOUS

Zig and Zag are two young executives who work for the same boss. One day the boss gave each of them a problem to solve. Being a no-nonsense guy, Zig figured out a solution, solved the problem and reported back to the boss that afternoon. The boss was glad to have the matter taken care of but figures it couldn't have been much of a problem if Zig handled it so quickly. So Zig got a polite thank-you and his effort was taken for granted.

Zag, on the other hand, is smoke blower *extraordinaire*. He learned long ago that the biggest rewards are not given for solving problems but for "analyzing and processing" them. So Zag attacked his problem by:

- Creating a file. When the boss asked how things were progressing, Zag replied, "I'm gathering documentation. I've got a file on it."
- Sending an obtuse, vaguely worded memo to everyone he could think of, asking them for "written input" on the matter.
- Hiring a consultant to study the problem in depth and write a lengthy report, which concluded that there should be more in-depth study and consultation.
- Appointing a standing committee which met regularly to discuss the problem and all of its ramifications.

• Convincing the boss to hold a weekend conference at a nice resort where the entire office could discuss the matter informally.

• Carefully selecting a task force of staff people who knew absolutely nothing about the problem and asking them for a thorough investigation.

• Directing the Data Processing Department to scan its files, print out reams of any data remotely related to the problem and send copies to all concerned.

Zag has taken to heart James H. Boren's advice to formal bureaucrats*:

> Implement, finalize, thrust, and embue;
> Interface, maximize, meet, and review;
> Orchestrate, optimize, test, and compute;
> Dialogue, quantitize, rate and refute.

Why does Zag behave this way? Once again, ask the magic question. By substituting analysis for action, Zag has three things going for him:

1. He takes no risk.

2. He creates high visibility and makes lots of good contacts throughout the company.

3. His boss loves it. "That Zag is a leader of the future. I gave him a tough problem to solve and he's leaving no stone unturned. In fact, I'll bet he has fifty people working on it by now."

If you think Zag is on his way to the top, forget it. He is not learning how to make decisions and take action. Sooner or later Zag's paralysis by analysis will cause him to be labeled as one who cannot make decisions and is therefore unfit to manage.

As for Zig, he will do one of two things:

1. Imitate Zag because the system has rewarded Zag's behavior.

---

*James H. Boren, *When in Doubt, Mumble* (New York: Van Nostrand Reinhold Company, 1972), p. 20.

2. Leave the company and go where his abilities are rewarded.

In either case the company loses.

Does your organization reward the Zigs or the Zags?

Too many large companies suffer from a shortage of entrepreneurship and an abundance of bullship. They are managed by people who know how to hold long meetings, hire consultants, write reports, analyze facts and figures and generate reams of paper, but who cannot choose a course of action and get on with it. To be sure, planning, foresight and analysis are important. But many of us seem to have forgotten something that is far more important:

THE PURPOSE OF ANY ORGANIZATION IS TO GET RESULTS

If you ask the people at the top what it takes to get there, one of their common answers is amazingly simple:

DECIDE ON WHAT YOU'RE GOING TO DO AND DO IT NOW!

Decisive people with the guts to act on their convictions almost always prevail simply because others are indecisive. In any organization you will find no shortage of people willing to analyze, verbalize and opinionize, but few who will be decisive. Most people simply don't have the assertiveness and self-confidence to put their career or reputation on the line when it's time to make decisions. This makes it incredibly simple for action-oriented types to rise to the top.

More important, good managers and organizations promote innovation and growth by giving their staff the freedom to decide and act. They don't waste precious time meeting, analyzing and forever putting decisions on hold. In essence, they tell their people, "Make up your mind and do it. If it isn't working out, either fix it or decide to do something else and do that. You won't be penalized for a bad decision, but you will be penalized for indecision."

Nevertheless, many of us have a terrible time when it comes to being decisive. If you or someone you know has this problem, the following ideas will help:

☐ 1. *Make decision making a habit.* You will make a few bad choices at first, but decision making, like most other things, gets better with practice. Experience will improve your judgment to the point where you'll be correct most of the time. And it's far better to be right 51 percent of the time than to get nothing at all done because you can't decide what to do.

☐ 2. *Don't tolerate reverse decision making.* Have you ever given someone a problem to solve only to have him drop it back in your lap? Don't put up with it. Tell him to write down as many solutions as he can think of, rank them in order of desirability and choose one or more. That way he will sharpen his decision-making skills and stop wasting your time.

☐ 3. *Write down the decision you have to make as clearly and simply as you can and set a deadline for making it.* Strip away the symptoms and write down only the heart of the problem. Allocate enough time (based on the importance of the decision) for gathering and analyzing information. Then make your choice by the deadline. This will keep you from falling into the trap of over-analyzing, vacillating and procrastinating.

☐ 4. *Obtain the best information you can within the time limits.* If you wait for the right amount of or the perfect information, you'll wait forever. President Harry Truman summed it all up by saying he made decisions by getting the best information available, deciding and telling his critics to go to hell.

☐ 5. *Brainstorm as many different alternatives as you can.* If you went to a business school, forget what you were taught about finding an optimal solution. How are you going to know when you have it? Just come up with as many solutions as you can and assign each one a point value from 1 to 10. Also realize that in the real world there will usually be at least several good options, and you may be able to choose any or all of them.

☐ 6. *If you need to further analyze alternatives, use the balance-sheet approach.* List all the advantages of a solution on the left side of a sheet of paper and all the disadvantages on the right side. Compare the pluses and minuses and make your decision. Benjamin Franklin proposed this idea over two hundred years ago and it's still excellent advice.

☐ 7. *Take action, or reward those who do.* As an anonymous executive said:

> To look is one thing. To see what you look at is another. To understand what you see is a third. To learn from what you understand is still something else. But to act on what you learn is all that really matters.

Reward Smart Work Instead of Busywork

The key to working smarter is knowing the difference between motion and direction.

—ANONYMOUS

Jeff, a plant manager, had an interesting philosophy about work:

IF YOU CAN'T DO YOUR JOB IN AN EIGHT-HOUR WORK DAY, THEN EITHER YOU HAVE TOO MUCH WORK ASSIGNED OR YOU'RE INCOMPETENT.

I must admit that when I first met Jeff I thought he was a little bit nuts. He would actually walk the halls every day five minutes after quitting time and throw out anyone who was still working. Nevertheless, things went smoothly, the plant ran at maximum capacity and morale was excellent for the three years he served as plant manager. It's hard to argue with success.

About four years ago Jeff was promoted and Jules was hired as his replacement. Jules's approach to work is: "An eight-hour day just isn't enough time if you really want to do your job effectively. Besides, anybody who leaves at quitting time can't be very dedicated. To move up in my organization you have to be a dedicated worker."

Not surprisingly, people started coming in earlier and leaving later, even though the workload was the same. Instead of arriving at 7:30 A.M. and leaving at 4 P.M., people started coming to work between 6:30 and 7:00 A.M. and staying until 5:00, 6:00 or sometimes even 7:00 P.M.

You might deduce that the longer work hours have resulted in higher productivity and a smoother-running plant due to a more "dedicated" work force. Wrong! The fact is that during the past four years plant production has actually declined, and the old-timers say that problems have been at an all-time high since Jules took over. To a man they complain about delays, bottlenecks and poor worker morale. And when you examine how they are spending their work days, the reason becomes obvious.

Early mornings are now times for social gatherings. Instead of coming in at 7:30 A.M. and getting down to business, everybody gets a nice hot cup of coffee, or two or three, and talks about what happened last night or what they have planned for the weekend. It is usually well after 8:00 A.M. before people settle down to work.

Afternoons are worse. Thirty-minute lunch breaks have evolved into two-hour marathons complete with drinks. By 4:00 P.M., when people have been at work eight or nine hours, concentration starts to fade. Many turn their attention to nonjob activities like making phone calls, doing homework for a night class or balancing their checkbook. When Jules appears, everybody makes an extra effort to look busy and dedicated.

There was a method to Jeff's madness of kicking people out at quitting time. He forced them to become goal-oriented. Everybody knew they had only eight hours in which to get things done, and they developed efficient and effective work habits. But Jules changed the work climate from *goal* oriented to *time* oriented. Once rewards were given for working long hours and looking busy, people developed all sorts of time-wasting behavior patterns to fill up the long work day, and productivity suffered.

Comedian Woody Allen once remarked that showing up is 80 percent of life. Some employees behave as if showing up and looking busy is 100 percent of work. Unfortunately, most of us are not rewarded for achieving specific goals that contribute to output. Instead, the rewards go for punching in and out at a certain time. Worse yet, like Jules, many managers assume the busiest people who work endless hours are the best workers and tend to reward them for busy behavior instead of results.

Ironically, people tend to look busiest when they don't know what they are trying to accomplish. Being busy becomes the goal that fills the void of purpose, as in the case of the husband taking a trip with his wife: After several hundred nonstop miles she looked at a map and said to him, "We're lost." "So what?" he replied. "We're making great time!"

If an NFL halfback ran feverishly from sideline to sideline and never gained a yard, he would be cut from the team. If an Olympic swimmer dived into the pool and simply splashed around, he would be an international laughingstock. If a baseball player hit only foul balls, he wouldn't stay on the team very long. Yet every day millions of white-collar and professional workers go to work and flounder just as badly because they don't clearly understand their job's goals and/or see no relationship between performance and rewards.

Not surprisingly, studies show that office efficiency consistently averages only 45 to 50 percent. And today's professional and white-collar workers represent 53 percent of the labor force and 70 percent of the national payroll. The busywork problem is not limited to white-collar jobs, but it is definitely more prevalent in offices than in factories.

The solution to the activity trap is to reward people for achieving specific, measurable goals rather than for showing up, looking busy and appearing to be totally dedicated, overworked souls. Reward acting and you get actors. Reward results and you get results.

In addition to rewarding goal achievement, here are several other useful strategies for converting actors into producers:

☐ 1. *Make sure you have the right person for the job.* People who lack either the ability or the training for a job will waste enormous amounts of time and energy trying to do what they simply cannot do. Lack of innate ability is *rarely* the problem when people fail to produce. Given the right amount of patience and motivation, most people can be trained to do most jobs very well.

☐ 2. *Give people the tools to do the job.* A worker is no better than his tools. Poor equipment means poor performance.

☐ 3. *Define each job's limits.* Everyone should have a clear understanding of where the boundaries of his job begin and end. Otherwise, people may needlessly duplicate each other's efforts while trying to do the same job.

☐ 4. *Make sure each person understands how his job contributes to the overall work effort.* This is important for two reasons. First, it increases motivation by showing people why their job is meaningful and important. And second, people who understand how their job contributes are much less likely to waste time going off on tangents.

☐ 5. *Give special attention to workers whose results fall short of their efforts.* They may have developed poor work habits. Tell them in a caring and helpful way that you want to see them do the best possible job while expending the least amount of time and effort. Point out that the rewards are for results—not for buckets of sweat, long hours, ulcers or nervous breakdowns. Send them to a good time management seminar* or have them read Action Plan 4 of this book.

☐ 6. *Encourage a quiet time.* People who get so busy that they don't have time to think are a liability to themselves and the organization. Ask everyone to invest a small amount of time each workday for solitary thinking, reflecting and planning. Ask them to use quiet time to consider the important goals of their job and how they are going to use today to help achieve them. Taking time each day to plan and put things in perspective greatly reduces needless busywork.

☐ 7. *Beware of proceduritis.* It's the scourge of modern-day bureaucracy. Procedurcrats are people who don't care *what* is being done, but rather *how* it is being done. For example, as soon as an important decision is on the floor at a meeting, the procedurcrat shifts the focus from what the decision ought to be to how the group should go about reaching it. He is the one who always says, "Let's make sure we're following all the right procedures." This usually results in a potentially unending procedural debate that detracts from the real reason the meeting

*One of my earlier books, *Working Smart* (McGraw-Hill Book Company, 1979, and available in paperback from Warner Books), deals exclusively with time management.

· was called. Procedurcrats waste a lot of time because they focus on how to achieve goals without focusing on what goals to achieve. Consequently, they usually end up doing the wrong things—but they do them very well.

☐ 8. *If people have finished their work, let them go home.* Assuming the nature of the job permits it, why keep people around if they have completed an agreed-on amount of satisfactory work? If you make them stay, they will just learn how to waste time and create problems for others. And time off is a great way to reward effective workers. Similarly, if people can do a better job at home on pet projects, let them stay home. In the final analysis, results are all that matter. Attendance and activity don't.

☐ 9. *Simplify*—the subject of the next strategy.

Reward Simplification Instead of Needless Complication

Good management is the art of making difficult things simple, not simple things difficult.

—ANONYMOUS

Marks and Spencer is Britain's largest clothing store chain. On a spring afternoon in 1956, Sir Simon Marks, chairman of the board, visited one store in Slough. He saw a sales clerk poring over a stock order form and asked, "What are you doing?" The clerk explained that he was filling out an intricate form to get goods moved from the stockrooms onto the shelves.

"What's it for? What use do you make of it?" Sir Simon asked.

"I'm not sure why we use it. It makes no sense to me, but it's the system," replied the clerk.

Sir Simon examined the complex form and couldn't understand it either. Moreover, he realized that while clerks filled out complicated forms, customers had to wait. So he promptly abolished the form and threw open the stockroom doors to the sales staff. Eliminating the form saved the company over $50,000 the first year in purchases of 2,500,000 forms. Better yet, the sales force became enthusiastic about their work. Said one salesperson, "We know our stock much better and we feel responsible for it. It's marvelous to be able to nip upstairs when your shelves get low, and it's a help, too, to know what's upstairs."

Sir Simon's visit to the Slough store was just the beginning.

Next, he and another director began studying the operations at two other stores. They questioned every detail of every form and procedure, asking, "What's this for?" "Do we really need that form?" "Why that card?" "Why? Why? Why?" They found mountains of unnecessary records that had the stores choking on red tape. As Sir Simon remarked, "One of our warehouse porters could get a visa to an Iron Curtain country more easily than he could get through our stockroom doors."

At this point Sir Simon decided it was time for companywide action. He announced a major campaign to simplify procedures and reduce paperwork. The slogan was "If in doubt, cut it out." A committee was created to examine every form and decide if its cost could be justified. If not, it had to go. Sir Simon himself spent countless days at the head office in London talking to nearly two thousand employees.

Everywhere Marks and Spencer looked, it found itself spending dollars to save pennies. In one office Sir Simon talked to three clerks who had spent an entire week checking if a statement for $2000 was correct. It wasn't. The railway owed them 20 cents! Sir Simon replaced the detailed checking with spot-checking and gave the clerks other work. In another instance, the central inventory listed the company's equipment in detail down to the last light bulb. "We refuse to pay five pence to move the safe to recover the sixpence that rolled under it," said Sir Simon. The central inventory was scratched.

Perfectionistic, detailed checking was replaced with sampling. Store managers were given the authority to make on-the-spot decisions and were held responsible for a reasonable return on investment. Sales clerks no longer had to be number recorders. With their jobs simplified, they learned new tasks more quickly and could devote more time to tending to customers. Within two years the company eliminated 22 million forms weighing 105 tons. Profits, morale and productivity soared.

As the simplification process went on, someone suggested doing away with time clocks. Several stores tried it and reported that punctuality improved! Removing the time clocks improved morale and saved the company a million time cards a year. Bimonthly, detailed inventories were eliminated at another store and replaced with estimates, sales-trend reports and detailed spot-checks as safeguards. This saved the store the cost of one worker a week, and the savings multiplied when it was adopted by all 237 stores.

By making a concerted effort to simplify its operations, Marks and Spencer did its stockholders, managers, employees and customers a huge favor. And it all started with Sir Simon asking a clerk one simple question: "What are you doing?"

When a new business begins, complexity is rarely a problem. But success usually leads to growth, and with growth comes complexity. And this is where most companies make a big mistake. They hire more people and create new systems and procedures to deal with the complexity—and things get more complicated. Yet the very essence of good management is keeping everything as simple as possible so people can do their jobs. It sounds paradoxical, but the more complex things get, the greater the need for simplicity.

Keeping things simple is very hard work. But good organizations and managers work hard to keep things simple and prevent goals from getting lost in the shuffle of daily activities. The basics of simplification can be summed up in three words:

ELIMINATE THE UNNECESSARY.

Yet, as pointed out earlier, most organizations fall into the trap of rewarding people who complicate matters and ignoring those who keep matters simple. Why not do the opposite? Trim organizations are responsive, flexible and better equipped to cope with change and pounce on opportunities. And fat organizations are unwieldy and may not be able to meet new or competitive challenges. Use the following simplification strategies to put more muscle and less fat in your operation:

☐ 1. *Simplify jobs.* Ask everyone who works for you (yourself included) to write the answers to the following questions in a total of 250 words (one page) or less:

- What results do I produce in my job?
- Why am I producing them?
- What am I doing that is unnecessary?

Answering these three simple questions will force everyone to go back to the basics of their job and consider how what they do contributes to output. If it does not contribute to output, it can be scratched.

☐   2. *Simplify structure.* Every six months Bill McGowan, founder and CEO of MCI Telecommunications Corporation, gives the following message to his newly hired managers: "I know some of you with your business-school backgrounds are out there already beginning to draw organization charts and write manuals for operating procedures. As soon as I find out who you are, I'm going to fire every last one of you." From the outset, McGowan makes it clear that people aren't going to keep their jobs by creating work for each other. Question every job and every level of management. Do you really need it? Can two levels be combined? Is every job worth more than it costs? Is it regularly contributing to output, or is it creating needless work? Such questions need to be asked regularly of every job. Remember, every time you add a level of management you hinder communication by removing the person at the bottom one more level from the person at the top. Well-run Japanese and American corporations are characterized by lean staffs and few levels of management. And the Catholic Church, one of the world's largest organizations, has only five levels of management between parish priest and Pope.

☐   3. *Simplify procedures and controls.* Several years ago Intel Corporation found itself a victim of bureaucracy. It took 95 steps and 12 pieces of paper to get a $2.79 pen from the stationery department. By using principles of work simplification, the 95 steps were reduced to eight and the 12 pieces of paper to one. In other applications of work simplification, Intel reduced the number of steps in its hiring procedure from 364 to 250 and reduced the number of minutes it took to process an accounts-payable voucher from 24 to 18.

There is no mystery or genius required to use work simplification. Simply take every procedure, break it into as many detailed steps as you can, chart them and question every step. Can you eliminate it, simplify it, combine two or more steps, or change the sequence of steps to make it more efficient? Office procedures, like weeds, have to be kept in check with regular thinning. And work simplification is a very helpful tool toward that end.*

☐ 4. *Simplify communication.* When speaking of a certain lawyer, Abraham Lincoln remarked, "He can compress the most words into the smallest ideas better than any man I ever met." As more of us assume information-producing jobs, there is going to be more information. And information overload is one sure way to immobilize people. We all need to work hard to keep our communication as simple and brief as possible. Keep all written communication to an absolute minimum. Question every line of every form, report and memorandum and ask, "Does this cause anyone to take any useful action?" If not, get rid of it. Communicate to others in language they understand. Question regular meetings and standing committees. Can any be eliminated, reduced or combined? Go over those volumes of computer printouts line by line. Pick out the information you need and ask the data-processing people to send you only what you need. Resolve to go through your reading matter by a certain date or get rid of it. You won't get ahead by reading yesterday's information today. Reduce your time on the telephone by having incoming calls screened, placing calls in batches and outlining what you want to discuss before you call. In short, focus on selecting, sending and receiving only the information that you and others need to get your work done and ignore the rest.

☐ 5. *Reward the simplifiers.* Some years ago a hospital employed a pharmacist who constantly overspent his budget. The problem was solved by freezing the budget and allowing the pharmacist to keep what he saved as a year-end bonus. Remember, if your business earns a 10 percent return on investment, every dollar saved through simplification is equal to ten dollars of increased revenue. Let people share in the savings, and give plenty of recognition and other appropriate rewards. One final word of caution: If you use simplification as a tool to furlough people, don't expect cooperation. One boss I know gives a bonus and a better job to anyone who can find a way to eliminate his own present job. That's making the most of GMP.

*For an excellent book on white-collar work simplification, see *Work Simplification* by Ralph E. Steere (Bureau of Business Practice, Waterford, Connecticut, 1979).

Reward Quietly Effective Behavior Instead of Squeaking Joints

The greatest ability is dependability.

—CURT BERGWALL

According to William Wilkerson, the anatomy of any organization includes four different kinds of bones:

- Wish-bones—who wish someone else would do the work.
- Jaw-bones—who talk a lot but do little else.
- Knuckle-bones—who knock what everyone else does.
- Back-bones—who get down and actually do the work.

Wherever you work I hope you are blessed with plenty of back-bones and few or none of the others. If not, maybe you can benefit from the experience of Jim, a sales manager.

"Another week shot to hell," Jim thought as he headed home one Friday evening. Reflecting on the week, he realized that practically all his time had been taken up resolving disputes, hearing complaints and listening to excuses from sales reps. One complained of having a bad territory, another about the bonus plan. Two others were arguing over how to split the commission on a joint sales effort. And still others spent hours of Jim's time telling him about their car problems, domestic problems or personal problems that had kept them from calling on accounts.

For the next several weeks Jim kept a written log of how much time he spent with each rep. The log revealed that 80 percent of his time was spent attending to low producers. Little, if any, time was being devoted to the best sales reps. He wondered what would happen if he devoted that much time and effort to helping the high producers and decided to give it a try.

From then on he started devoting 80 percent of his time to the top third of the sales force. He coached them, helped them, listened to them, praised them, thanked them and urged them on with plenty of positive strokes. Another 15 percent of his time was spent recruiting new reps to replace those who left. And the remaining small amount of time was given to reps whose productivity was average or less.

Needless to say, Jim's new policy wasn't a big hit with the lower producers. Many complained even louder and some left. But Jim just refused to pay much attention to anyone until they produced good results.

The first result Jim noticed was a sharp increase in total sales. The better reps thrived on the positive stroking and sold even more. Some of the previously low producers jumped into the top third so they could once again enjoy the boss's attention. By focusing his efforts on the high performers, Jim got better results than when he tried to help everyone. The policy worked well for a number of years.

Every organization needs quiet heroes—reliable people who know their jobs and do them without calling a lot of attention to themselves. But too often the deeds of quiet heroes are drowned out by squeaking joints who spend their time creating problems instead of results. Managers, being problem solvers, get sucked into the trap of reinforcing squeaking joints by paying attention to them and helping solve their problems. All of which leaves little time to devote to the better producers who end up feeling neglected.

Most people don't mind working hard, but they do mind having their efforts taken for granted. It makes them feel used, discouraged, exploited and unappreciated. And when that happens, they fight back by withholding effort or engaging in counterproductive pastimes.

I once saw a little girl walking home from kindergarten with a large, round, paper button pinned to her dress that read:

CATCH ME BEING GOOD.

That button was sending a very important message from the teacher to the girl's parents that said, in effect: "If you only pay attention to her when she misbehaves, you're reinforcing bad behavior. But if you praise and reward her when she's good, you'll get more good behavior and help her develop into the person you want her to be."

To be sure, employees are not children, and I am not suggesting they be treated as such. But children and employees are people, and people do whatever it takes to get others to recognize them. Managers who ignore quiet heroes and spend their time oiling squeaking joints may soon find everyone squeaking.

To encourage more quietly effective behavior, keep these points in mind:

☐ 1. *Consciously work at identifying and acknowledging good behavior.* In your mind's eye, imagine that those at work are wearing a "catch me being good" button whenever you see them. I'm not suggesting that you compliment and reward everyone whenever you see good behavior. If you do, people will think you have lost your marbles. Make a list of the people you work with and what you like about what they do. When the time is right, tell each one specifically what you like about their work and encourage them to do even better. Good behavior is too precious to be taken for granted.

☐ 2. *Seek out your quiet heroes and resolve to spend time encouraging and rewarding them.* It's so easy to overlook dependable people. But they are the nucleus of any successful organization. Answering the following questions will help you identify them:

- Who is rarely, if ever, absent?
- Who works well under pressure?
- Who consistently turns out high-quality work on time?
- Who is willing to give a second effort when the team needs it?
- Who can you count on to take up the slack in someone else's absence?
- Who doesn't constantly pester others for advice and guidance?

- Who is so quiet and unassuming that you hardly know he's there except for his good work?
- Who can be trusted to work just as well in the boss's absence?
- Who produces many more answers than problems?
- Who helps others to do their jobs better?
- Who regularly strives to improve his work?
- Who smooths out conflicts, fosters cooperation and builds morale?
- In short, who is there whenever you need him?

Another reward that will keep your quiet heroes motivated is to take a sincere interest in them—not only as employees, but as human beings. Listen to them. What are their hopes, fears, likes, dislikes, joys and frustrations, both on and off the job? Be ready and willing to help them with their problems and reassure them when they have self-doubts. Taking a personal interest in people builds the bonds of trust necessary for good teamwork. It is one essential ingredient of every successful manager I have ever known.

☐ 3. *Keep alert for squeaking joints and don't oil them.* Did you notice how Jim changed the performance of his sales force? He didn't lecture, beg or plead with them. He changed his behavior to reward the high producers with his time and attention and they got the message. Rewards and your own behavior in making rewards are the best ways to teach people what you expect from them.

For example, don't spend your time helping people solve crises they intentionally create. Instead, tell them it is their responsibility and add it to their regular workload. Don't refuse to give work to those who intentionally screw up because they think you will give it to a quiet hero. Expect them to do it and hold them accountable. If you decide a person is a chronic complainer without legitimate grounds, ignore him. Don't waste your time with game players who are forever thinking up ways to be unproductive. Keep the focus of your behavior on expecting and rewarding the behavior you want from others. As Henrik Ibsen said, "A thousand words will not leave so deep an impression as one deed."

☐ 4. *When you have to give criticism remember this rule:*

PRAISE THE WORKER, CRITICIZE THE WORK.

None of us enjoys having holes poked in our work after we have invested time, effort and emotion in it. Nevertheless, pointing out errors and needed corrections is an essential part of a manager's job. When you have to be critical, be careful. Like walking through a minefield, one bad step can do irreparable harm.

Never begin your criticism by pointing out what is wrong. That puts people on the defensive, and defensive people don't listen. Instead, start out by praising the good points of the work and saying how you appreciate the person's effort and ability. Then shift the focus to what needs to be done to make things right or to keep them from going wrong in the future. Finally, end the discussion by again praising the person for his efforts, offering your support and expressing your confidence in him.

If someone is goofing off and not doing the work expected, be more direct. Tell him how disappointed his work makes you feel because you know he is capable of doing a much better job. Then get to the specifics of what you expect from him in no uncertain terms and give him a deadline for doing it. End the discussion by offering your support and telling him, "You're much better than this."

A constructive critique leaves others with an understanding of the errors, the means to correct them, a feeling of appreciation and an eagerness to improve. Before delivering your criticism, be sure it can provide those four things.

In the shuffle of everyday business it is only natural to overlook good behavior and tend to the bad. But can you afford it? The next time you are tempted to overlook a quiet hero, remember these words from Samuel Goldwyn: "Dammit, couldn't you *hear* me keeping quiet?"

Reward Quality Work Instead of Fast Work

The best preparation for tomorrow is to do today's work superbly well.

—SIR WILLIAM OSLER

In our busy, "instant" society we put a premium on fast work. Everybody wants everything yesterday. But all too often the results are shoddy work and second-rate goods and services. The following poem from an anonymous author is a vivid portrayal of:

The Rush Job

I am a rush job.
I belong to no age, for men have always hurried.
I prod all human endeavor. Men believe me necessary—
　　but falsely.
I rush today because I was not planned yesterday.
I demand excessive energy and concentration.
I override obstacles, but at great expense.
I illustrate the old saying "Haste makes waste."
My path is strewn with the evils of overtime, mistakes and
　　disappointment.
Accuracy and quality give way to speed.
Ruthlessly I rush on . . .
I am a rush job.

Traditional attempts to improve productivity have usually focused on finding answers to two questions:

1. How can we do it faster?
2. How can we do it cheaper?

But in our effort to do things faster and cheaper we overlooked a third and more basic question:

3. How can we do it right the first time?

As we have learned from the Japanese (who originally
learned it from us), the key to higher productivity lies in working better rather than faster. Working faster and cheaper only
allows you to produce the same old defects more efficiently. But
improving quality has a number of large, long-run payoffs:

> • *Lower costs.* Doing things right the first time lowers the
> cost of materials, inspection, repair and warranties. Auto
> industry sources estimate that as much as 25 percent of the
> price of an American car is attributable to poor quality.
> Before making a commitment to improve quality, Hewlett-
> Packard calculated that as much as 25 percent of its man-
> ufacturing assets were tied up in reacting to quality prob-
> lems. By learning to do things right the first time, large
> companies like IBM are saving an estimated $5 to $10
> million per month. Quality expert Phil Crosby says it best:
> "Quality is free. What costs money are the unquality
> things—all the actions that involve not doing jobs right
> the first time." Consultants estimate that as much as 40
> percent of the cost of manufacturing in the United States is
> associated with not doing jobs right the first time.
> • *Higher output.* Doing things right the first time makes
> previously wasted resources productive. Managers devote
> less time to inspecting and more to productive activities.
> Workers spend time producing instead of repairing and
> reworking. Previously wasted energy and materials are
> channeled into finished goods and services.
> By boosting quality, you automatically get things done
> faster and cheaper. But the next two large payoffs make
> quality even more valuable.
> • *Worker pride.* Doing things right the first time creates

the positive feelings of confidence and success that come from mastering a job and doing it well. Better yet, it motivates people to try even harder. Yet how many times have you heard workers told, "Just get it done on time." This robs them of the opportunity to do their best. More important, management is ignoring a free reward to use to increase productivity.

• *Customer loyalty.* The average business spends about six times more to attract new customers than it does to keep old ones. But doing things right every time is the surest path to getting repeat business and attracting new customers. Moreover, consumer research trends suggest that customers will demand increasingly higher levels of quality in the future. Quality, not price, is what consumers value most in a product, and they are willing to pay extra for it. On the other hand, poor quality is the quickest route to losing customers. As a sign in a bicycle shop said it best: "The bitterness of poor quality lingers long after the sweetness of a cheap price is forgotten."

Now that you know the advantages of quality you're probably thinking, "That's great, but who can do things right all the time?" Given that we know how and want to, all of us can.

For example, during World War II the U.S. government discovered its parachutes failed to open 5 percent of the time. Clearly, nothing less than zero defects was an acceptable level of quality. How do you tell paratroopers going on a mission that one out of twenty of the parachutes is not going to open? The problem was solved by requiring parachute packers and inspectors to put on one of their products occasionally and jump out of a plane. Parachute quality quickly improved from 95 to 100 percent.

How many babies is a maternity ward nurse allowed to drop? How many bad brake jobs would you allow your mechanic to perform? What is an acceptable failure rate for the engineer who designs suspension bridges? How many faulty heart bypass operations is a surgeon allowed? How many mistakes do you allow your company to make in your paycheck? As you can see, quality is really a matter of attitude and commitment.

Why are most businesses hurting for quality? Ask the magic question. The reward system is structured to encourage quantity instead of quality. We are so obsessed with how much gets done that we neglect how well it is done. And we're paying a huge price for our negligence with a gigantic trade deficit, loss of worker pride, wasted time, effort and materials, and products and services that are less than they could be. We are short-changing ourselves and each other by giving less than our best.

Getting a commitment to quality, like anything else, starts with rewarding it—not just on the factory floor, but from the highest levels of management on down. Unless top management has a vested, ongoing interest in better quality, no lasting improvement is likely to be made.

It's easy to blame workers, tools and materials for poor quality because they are readily visible, but it's also a huge mistake. One hundred percent of all quality problems and solutions start with top management. As Ray Boedecker, IBM's director of quality, put it, "When the CEO says, 'Let's go. Let's learn. Let's do it.'—that's when quality begins. It's the single most compelling, motivating factor."

Companies with a serious commitment to improving quality are gaining management support in numerous ways. Here are a few:

- At Texas Instruments about one hundred top level managers are ranked and told how they rank on quality performance. The ranking is factored into raises and bonuses.
- If a Chrysler plant fails to meet quality goals for one week, the manager must submit a written explanation and solution. Missing goals for a month means being called before a high-level executive committee to give an explanation.
- At Nashua Corporation, up to 40 percent of an executive's bonus is based on quality.
- Executive promotions at CBS Records are decided by comparing the quality of the products with that of competitors' products in seven different catagories. To ensure objectivity, comparisons are made by computer.

• Senior executives at Goodyear wear blimp-shaped tiepins that read "Quality starts here."

• Pitney Bowes, Inc., encourages quality competitions among plants and employees, giving monetary rewards and a hero's recognition to the winners.

Once management gets serious about quality, several other factors are necessary to ensure that quality improvement becomes an ongoing reality and not just another fad:

☐ 1. *Every employee needs to understand what quality is and is not.* Everybody thinks they know what quality is—but most do not. The following are points that everyone needs to understand:

QUALITY IS:	QUALITY IS NOT:
1. Conforming to preset, measurable standards of performance.	1. Telling people to do their best.
2. A total, ongoing program and a commitment to do things right the first time every time.	2. A goal to be set, reached, and forgotten.
3. Proper planning and design to prevent defects before they occur.	3. The inspection, detection and correction of defects.
4. Measured by calculating the cost of quality (the cost of not doing things right the first time).	4. Measured by subjective evaluations.

☐ 2. *Train* everybody *in the basics of statistical quality control, starting at the very top.* The greatest obstacle to using quality-control techniques is the belief that they are too difficult for the average person to understand. This is simply not true. Anybody who can read a simple chart or learn to do basic arithmetic can learn how to understand and use quality-control techniques. The seeds of Japan's rise from junk merchant to quality leader were planted when American quality-control experts taught their techniques to high-level Japanese executives and officials in 1950. Each level of management, in turn, taught it to the next lower level, until everyone from the bottom up understood and used quality-control techniques to measure performance.

☐ 3. *Spread the enthusiasm with communication, goals and rewards.* Can you post a quality scoreboard or bulletin board? How about a quality newsletter? How about a contest between departments for quality improvement, complete with worthwhile rewards? As for the goal, it should always be the same—zero defects. Do it right the first time.

☐ 4. *Ask the person who does the job how to improve it.* This is the basic idea behind quality circles. Odds are that the person who does the job knows more about it than anyone else, but that person is usually the last to be asked. People today are more eager to be involved in their work than ever. Seek out their ideas for improvement and reward them for those ideas.

☐ 5. *Treat your customers like lifetime partners.* You will create a situation in which your profits will grow and your customers will continue to be satisfied. Isn't that what quality is all about?

Reward Loyalty Instead of Turnover

You can buy a man's time; you can buy his physical presence at a given place; you can even buy a measured number of his skilled muscular motions per hour. But you cannot buy enthusiasm. . . . You cannot buy loyalty. . . . You cannot buy the devotion of hearts, minds or souls. You must earn these.

—CLARENCE FRANCIS

"I just don't understand why today's young people aren't more committed to work. When I was their age I was grateful just to have a job."

"George is a competent professor but he lacks a serious commitment to the university."

"Ellen was an excellent book rep but never had a serious commitment to publishing."

"Dr. LeBoeuf, how can we get our people more committed to the long-range success of our company?"

Have you noticed in recent years how often the word "commitment" comes up in conversations? Managers are forever talking about the need for greater employee loyalty and commitment. For what it's worth, my observation is that commitment is a lot like sex:

1. Everybody wants it.
2. Those who talk the most about it are probably getting the least of it.
3. It's impossible to get it without giving it.

"Never get married to a company because no company is married to you," said a father to his recently graduated son.

Every organization needs loyalty, but few actually reward it. Instead, they hire, fire and furlough people according to current economic needs. Worse yet, many companies actually teach people to be disloyal. Have you ever worked for an organization where the most recently hired are the best paid? Have you ever worked for a company where the way to get a raise or promotion is to get a better offer from elsewhere and threaten to leave? Have you ever worked for a company that promised great opportunities for advancement but filled the best job openings with outsiders? In most careers the greatest rewards are for changing jobs rather than remaining loyal to one company. Does it have to be that way? Not at all.

Fortunately, some companies treat people differently. They know that an ongoing, enthusiastic, committed work force is the key to continuous success and the surest road to preventing the high long-range costs of unionization and turnover. And they are smart enough to realize and practice this one simple principle:

YOU GET LOYALTY AND COMMITMENT FROM PEOPLE BY GIVING IT TO THEM.

If you doubt that, try this experiment: Find people who have been with a firm at least ten years and are still very excited and dedicated to the company. (Delta Air Lines employees are my favorite.) Ask them why they take so much pride and feel so much loyalty to the company. You will most likely get a number of answers, but they all will boil down to this: *They belong to an organization that cares about them, challenges them, believes in them and wants the best for them, not just as employees but as total human beings.*

If you ask, they will also tell you that the company demands plenty of time, effort and loyalty in return. Organizations that give a lot demand a lot. But isn't reciprocity the basis of all good relationships? In the final analysis, loyalty begets loyalty, trust begets trust, friendship begets friendship, and commitment begets commitment. It's that simple.

Employee loyalty and dedication don't just happen. Management has to make them happen. Creating a climate of loyalty, caring and trust is expensive, but the benefits are priceless. Here are the basics:

☐ 1. *Provide job security.* "When I first came to the United States, I thought how convenient it was for American employers to be able to lay off people whenever business slumped," said Sadami Wada, vice-president of Sony Corporation of America. But Wada soon changed his mind. "Now I understand why some American companies fail to gain the loyalty and dedication of their employees. Employees cannot care for an employer who is prepared to take their livelihood away at the first sign of trouble."

How loyal would you feel toward your parents had they thrown you out during hard times? Providing job security is not just a pipe dream—it's good business. Layoffs are very expensive and prevent companies from attracting and keeping good people who demand job stability. Such companies as IBM, Hewlett-Packard, Delta Air Lines and many others have followed a no-layoff policy for years and swear by it. Instead of laying off people, a company can weather an economic crisis by:

- Cutting pay across the board.
- Shortening the work week.
- Retraining and redeploying people whose jobs are eliminated.
- Loaning employees temporarily to other firms.
- Instituting a job-sharing program, where two employees fill one job.
- Providing lump-sum payments to people who will volunteer to resign or take early retirement.
- Bringing back into the company work that is being done by outsiders such as vendors, consultants and suppliers.
- Using idle workers to work on long-range maintenance, planning and problem-solving projects.

Job security alone will not build the sense of loyalty and commitment needed for long-range success. Nevertheless, it is the first essential step to creating a loyal, stable team.

☐ 2. *Build trust by keeping channels of communication open and clear.*

Companies with the highest morale and the least turnover are the ones that keep their people informed about goals and policies and listen to them. For example, Delta Air Lines employees meet with top management in groups of twenty-five to thirty at least once in every eighteen months. Attending each meeting is one of Delta's top nine policy makers, the appropriate vice-president and members of middle management. After a formal briefing of Delta events, the group's supervisor is excused and the floor is open for discussion. As one seventeen-year-old employee put it, "We can talk to them and they listen." Through this dialogue, top management is able to spot and solve problems at the source, get new ideas for improving operations and create a personal rapport with everyone in the company.

Additionally, Delta has an open-door policy that allows any employee to discuss a problem with any level of management without going through hierarchy channels or fearing repercussions. If a maintenance employee needs to see the president, he can. The president will see to it that the problem is looked into and the employee told what was found and/or done.

☐ 3. *Promote from within.* Promoting insiders to good jobs sends a loud and clear message to everyone that loyalty is rewarded. Hiring outsiders for choice positions says just the opposite.

☐ 4. *Invest in the long-term growth and development of people.* Promotion from within is a disaster if people are not groomed to assume positions of greater responsibility. Companies with loyal employees invest heavily in the continuous education, training and development of their people.

To be sure, training and development are expensive. But if you think education is expensive, try ignorance. Sooner or later a company pays the cost of training through employees' mistakes, through higher salaries to attract those already trained or through time spent training the people it has. The last way breeds competence and loyalty.

☐ 5. *Pay and benefits must be perceived as fair.* It's easy to be pressured into paying the highest salaries to new employees in areas where skilled workers are in short supply. But the long-term result is disastrous. It ultimately leads to horrible morale, poor performance and high turnover among long-standing employees. Pay top dollar to your senior team-players. Like promotion from within, fair pay and benefits send the message to everyone that loyalty is rewarded.

☐ 6. *In short, treat people the way you would like to be treated.* People who are treated as if they are the key to the company's success become just that.

Reward Working Together Instead of Working Against

I know that I am among civilized men because they are fighting so savagely.

—VOLTAIRE

A man touring a mental institution was surprised to find only three guards watching over one hundred dangerous patients. "Aren't you afraid they will overpower you and escape?" he asked.

"No," replied one of the guards. "Lunatics never unite."

How united are the people where you work? Do they:

- Try to build up the importance of their own work and downplay the importance of others'?
- Refuse to fully extend a helping hand to each other when it is needed to get the job done?
- Spend lots of time sniping, backbiting, criticizing each other and playing political games?
- Form personal rivalries and "us versus them" group factions that disagree over just about everything?

If you nodded your head in agreement with most of those questions, chances are that the reward system where you work is structured to pay off one person or group at the expense of others. And a reward system that produces few winners at the cost of many losers is asking for trouble. For example:

• A bank decided to motivate its branch managers by having them compete with each other. A bonus was promised to the manager whose branch produced the most improved results. But the plan backfired. The bank discovered an officer steering customers to a particular branch to help that branch manager win the bonus.

• A computer company sponsored a sales contest only to find a Texas area rep poaching on the Oklahoma rep's turf.

• A photocopier salesman was caught asking customers to sign up for copiers even though they had no intention of going through with the deal. Why? The rep wanted to win the trip to Hawaii.

• A plant manager tried to improve productivity by pitting the day shift against the night shift and giving the winners an extra week's vacation. The plan had the opposite effect. Each shift tried to sabotage the other by jamming the machinery, hiding tools and reducing the materials inventory to near zero at the end of their respective shifts.

Competition and even conflict and confrontation can play a large role in any organization and may be a very healthy stimulus. Yet in the final analysis every organization is a team whose success depends on people working together to achieve common goals. And misplaced conflict and competition can literally destroy an organization.

Any outfit can survive a few troublemakers who thrive on creating unnecessary conflicts, but if wholesale adversity exists, the reward system probably encourages conflict and confrontation instead of teamwork.

For example, consider the traditional "us versus them" conflict between management and labor. Why does it exist? Ask the magic question. One key reason this adversary relationship has continued in some industries is that all parties are rewarded for conflict and confrontation. The workers' reward is higher wages, benefits and better working conditions. Managers, in turn, award themselves raises because managers have to make more than workers. The union prospers by staying in business as long as management and labor disagree. No disharmony, no union. Until foreign competition entered the picture, all parties could join in the conflict, reap the rewards and simply pass the costs on to the customer. But those days are over.

Someone once remarked, "If we didn't have the Japanese to compete with we would have had to invent them." Indeed, one of the best lessons to be learned from Japan is the proper use of teamwork and competition to increase productivity. In Japan heavy competition is encouraged between companies to produce the best possible products for the world market. But within companies and work groups, harmony, teamwork and cooperation take precedence. One of their favorite slogans is "None of us is as smart as all of us."

Teamwork rarely, if ever, happens by accident. It occurs when management makes it a priority and structures the work and the organization in ways that encourage cooperation. In short, if you want stars, reward your stars. But if you want team players, reward teamwork. Here are some practical ideas for team building that others have used successfully.

☐ 1. *Create self-managed work teams.* Time and again it has been shown that the creation of autonomous work groups can result in higher morale, productivity and teamwork. Here are the basics:

- Assign each team a significant piece of the work.
- Arrange the work environment to foster plenty of communication and interaction between members of the same team.
- Make the jobs interdependent. Each worker's job should be like a puzzle piece: only if all contribute can the job be completed successfully. This creates positive peer pressure and lessens the chances of anyone slacking off.
- Make sure every team member knows how to do all the jobs performed by the team. This makes each member more valuable, strengthens the team and allows for job rotation to reduce boredom.
- Give each team a meaningful way to measure and evaluate its performance—jobs per man hour, speed of

delivery, defects per thousand units, etc. With a way to keep score, each team can set specific benchmarks for measuring its own productivity, quality and other meaningful indicators.

• Ask team members to evaluate each other as part of each worker's job evaluation.

☐ 2. *Curtail misplaced competition.* If you find individuals or groups working against each other when they should be working together, here are a number of things you can do:

• Create a common goal with rewards that can be achieved only by working together.

• Identify the rewards for working against each other and remove them.

• Create or identify a common threat or enemy such as another company or a division (one that cannot be interfered with).

• Call the game. If two or more people (or groups) are sniping and playing political games with each other, put an immediate stop to it. Left to itself, misplaced conflict can spread like the plague. Meet with all parties at once, face to face, and get the issues out in the open. Ask them, "How is all this going to help anybody or the company?" This may help uncover counterproductive rewards. Point out that from now on the name of the game is cooperation and that they will be rewarded for it.

☐ 3. *Prevent future competition.* The best medicine is preventive medicine because you don't have to cure nonexistent illnesses. Here are some ways to prevent the problems of misplaced competition before they start:

• Reward people and groups on the basis of how they contribute to the group or the organization as a whole.

• Reward people and groups for the help they give each other.

• Stimulate frequent interaction between members of groups.

• Don't allow groups or individuals to become with-drawn and isolated from each other; encourage communication.

• Where possible, rotate members among groups.

• Avoid setting up win-lose competitions between individuals and groups where cooperation is crucial.

☐ 4. *Build teamwork with pride and recognition.* Two of the greatest team builders of this century are coaches Joe Paterno of Penn State and the late Paul Bear Bryant of Alabama. They speak from experience. Here are Coach Paterno's thoughts on pride:

> You make people feel that they're with a special company, a special institution that's worth making sacrifices for. If you're the kind of guy we call the "we and us" people that can work with the group by being unselfish, benefits will accrue to you. . . . By making sacrifices, if you're good, you're going to get it back a hundred times. I think you have to get that point across. If you have pride in your organization you can get people to do anything.

And here are Coach Bryant's words on recognition:

> I'm just a plowhand from Arkansas, but I have learned how to hold a team together. How to lift some men up, how to calm down others, until finally they've got one heartbeat together, a team. There's just three things I'd ever say:
>
> If anything goes bad, I did it.
> If anything goes semi-good, then we did it.
> If anything goes real good, then you did it.
>
> That's all it takes to get people to win football games for you.

☐ 5. *Use the "most important words" in communicating with your team.* As you work to build cooperation and trust, keep these points in mind:

• The six most important words in our language are "I admit I made a mistake."

• The five most important words are "You did a good job."

• The four most important words are "What is your opinion?"

• The three most important words are "Let's work together."

• The two most important words are "Thank you."

• The single most important word is "We."

Post those words on a bulletin board where everyone can see and begin using them. How we communicate has a lot to do with how we cooperate. Many people believe that tactful, polite communication is nothing but a lot of wind. But, as Marshal Foch once noted, "There is nothing but wind in a tire, but it makes riding in a car very smooth and pleasant."

Summing Up Part II

You have just learned ten types of behavior to reward and ten types of behavior not to reward.

REWARD	INSTEAD OF
1. Solid solutions	1. Quick fixes
2. Risk taking	2. Risk avoiding
3. Applied creativity	3. Mindless conformity
4. Decisive action	4. Paralysis by analysis
5. Smart work	5. Busywork
6. Simplification	6. Needless complication
7. Quietly effective behavior	7. Squeaking joints
8. Quality work	8. Fast work
9. Loyalty	9. Turnover
10. Working together	10. Working against

Now you're probably asking *how* you reward the ten important kinds of behavior. There are ten different ways to reward good work, and they are the subject of our first action plan in Part III.

PART III

ACTION

Part II was strategy; it taught you what to reward. Part III is tactics and action; it tells you who and how to reward. With a complete program of specific exercises and information, this final section guides you through a step-by-step process for using GMP to get the best from others, your boss and yourself.

As you read the techniques for managing with GMP, keep this point in mind: Getting better results always involves finding the correct answers to three crucial questions:

1. What behavior do I want?
2. How will I recognize it?
3. How will I reward it?

The Ten Best Ways to Reward Good Work

> *Do not refuse a wing to the person who gave you the whole chicken.*
>
> —R. G. H. SIU

Thus far you have learned GMP, the magic question and ten important kinds of behavior to reward. Now here are the ten best ways to reward those ten important kinds of behavior.

Reward #1: Money

Did you hear about the clothing manufacturer who turned out thousands of sweatshirts with "Money isn't everything" printed on them? He went bankrupt. In the world of work, money is power, prestige, security and *the* yardstick of success.

Some authorities argue that money is an overrated incentive. I thoroughly disagree. The problem is that *pay is not meaningfully linked to performance in most jobs*. Furthermore, the progressive income tax undermines rewarding pay for performance. Why work overtime if half of it goes to the government?

Nevertheless, companies that give monetary rewards based on performance get performance. Lincoln Electric Company of Cleveland pays most of its 2500 employees strictly on a piece-work and bonus system. Workers with two or more years of service are guaranteed at least 30 hours of work per week and each person is personally responsible for the quality of his own work. Any defects must be corrected by the worker on his own time and defects discovered by customers or quality control lower his bonus pay. Although workers complain about the hectic pace, Lincoln has no unions and turnover is under 4 percent per year.* In good years, workers have averaged over $45,000 per year, when the average manufacturing wage was just slightly over $18,000 per year. The message is clear: Pay for performance and you get performers; pay peanuts and you get monkeys.

Reward #2: Recognition

Author Laurence Peter said it best: "There are two kinds of egotists: Those who admit it and the rest of us." While money can be a very powerful incentive, recognition can be even more powerful. It sometimes costs little or nothing and, like money, almost everyone responds to it. It is amazing how hard people will work when the payoff is feeling appreciated and important.

How do you reward with recognition? Use your imagination and you will come up with plenty of ideas to fit the people where you work. But to get you started, here are some of the more popular ways to hand out those all-important "atta boys":

- Employee-of-the-month awards for highest sales, quality, productivity, most improvement, least absenteeism or whatever you designate as most important.
- Certificates, citations, trophies and plaques for achieving important goals.
- Clubs with special privileges for high achievers, such as million-dollar round-table clubs in the insurance industry.
- Favorable publicity, such as a write-up in the company or local newspaper.
- Changes in job title.
- Public praise for a job well done.
- A congratulatory letter for special achievement that goes in the employee's file.

---

* The average turnover in United States manufacturing jobs is approximately 4 percent per month!

- Special praise or attention from top management.
- Honors or awards presented at banquets.
- Publicly announced bonuses and raises.
- Status symbols such as rings, tiepins, a better office, cars and private parking spaces.
- A hall of fame with names and photographs of high achievers.
- Charts or posters showing how well an employee or group is doing the job.

"There are two things people want more than sex and money . . . recognition and praise." That's the gospel according to Mary Kay Ash, a lady who admits to knowing nothing about finance. Yet she has managed to turn an idea into a cosmetics empire that earned $600 million in 1983. How did she do it? Ask the magic question.

The reward system at Mary Kay Cosmetics is based on pay for performance and super-recognition for super-performance. Top saleswomen for Mary Kay earn up to $400,000 per year, and her top fifty sales reps averaged $100,000 per year in 1983. But the crown jewel of the Mary Kay reward system is the annual Awards Night, when 8000 women who sell Mary Kay cosmetics are showered with applause, praise and gifts ranging from pocket calculators to pink Cadillacs. Queens of sales and recruitment are crowned and presented with flowers and scepters, accompanied by standing ovations and musical fanfares.

Speaking in New Orleans to a group of broadcast owners and managers, Mary Kay said, "It's up to you to decide how to speak to your people. Do you single out individuals for public praise and recognition? I presume you won't want to give away pink Cadillacs, diamond rings and mink coats. But make people who work for you feel important. If you honor and serve them, they'll honor and serve you."

Reward #3: Time Off

This can be a very powerful incentive—especially with younger workers who want the freedom to pursue off-the-job activities. And it's a great way to keep people from forming time-wasting habits. Basically, there are three ways you can use time off as a reward:

1. If the job permits it, simply give people a job, a deadline and specify the quality you expect. If they finish before the deadline, the extra time is their reward.

2. If the job is one where they have to be there all day, you can still use time off as a reward. Specify an amount of work you want done by a certain time. If the work is completed on time satisfactorily, reward them with an afternoon, day or week off. Or you can set up a scoring system where people earn an hour off for maintaining a certain rate of output for a specific period of time. When they earn four hours, they can have a half day off; eight hours, a day off; etc.

3. You can award time off for improvements in quality, safety, teamwork or any behavior you feel is important.

Reward #4: A Piece of the Action

It's such a simple, practical idea:

EMPLOYEES WHO BECOME OWNERS
BEHAVE LIKE OWNERS.

Those who own a part of the company and have a stake in its success are far less likely to behave in ways that hurt productivity and profits. As Senator Russell Long so aptly put it, "I am convinced that for capitalism to continue to work in America, more Americans must be capitalists. It is natural that a worker who owns part of his company is going to be motivated to do a good job." Not surprisingly, a University of Michigan study found that firms with some worker ownership averaged profits one and a half times those of conventional companies in their field.

While many companies have employee stock-ownership plans, People Express Airlines has carried it a step farther. To be hired, a potential employee must buy stock in the firm. After buying stock and joining the company, he participates in a generous profit-sharing plan that distributes profits each quarter. There are no supervisory employees because they are not needed. All employees are sufficiently motivated to manage themselves.

A successful employee-ownership program depends heavily on the following key guidelines:

- The greater the percentage of employee ownership, the more employees should be involved in making decisions that affect their work.
- The adversarial relationship between labor and management must give way to cooperation. Everyone must learn to give a little in the interest of long-range prosperity.
- The company must produce a competitive, marketable product. All the employee-ownership plans in the world will not restore the United States steel and auto industries to their former size.
- Employee ownership should be in voting stock. Unless employees can vote their stock, they aren't owners.
- Employee owners need to realize that ownership carries with it basic responsibilities, i.e., patience and hard work.

Rewarding people with a piece of the action is no cure for poor management. But when carried out as part of a well-planned program of employee participation it can give a real boost to morale and productivity.

Reward #5: Favorite Work

Give people more of the tasks they enjoy doing as a reward for good performance. At the same time, excuse them from assignments they dislike. Since people usually enjoy doing the things they do best, this is a great way to improve the performance of your best performers. In essence, you say to them, "Tell me what you like to do best, do it well, and I'll give you more of the same. At the same time I'll excuse you from those certain jobs you least enjoy."

Reward #6: Advancement

I wish I had a dollar for every time I heard someone say, "I left the company because I felt I had gone as far as I could go."

Companies lose some of their best performers to other firms that offer greater responsibility, a bigger challenge and more opportunity to advance. The people you want to keep most are those the competition is most eager to hire.

The traditional way to reward with advancement is to give a full-fledged promotion up the managerial ladder. But if promotion isn't possible, perhaps you can reward with a special assignment or new responsibilities through which the employee can gain valuable experience. Or a lateral transfer to a new job where the employee can broaden his expertise could be another way to reward good performance.

One company with a promotion bottleneck kept a young manager by volunteering him to a government committee in Washington as a public service. He stayed on the company payroll, and when he returned, the bottleneck had opened up and he was promoted.

If nonmanagerial specialists (such as computer people, engineers and scientists) are crucial to company success, it is a good idea to establish a separate career ladder, complete with titles, pay and privileges for each level. Then technical people can continue to do what they do best and advance without having to become managers.

Reward #7: Freedom

Freedom and automony can be very effective rewards in jobs that have been tightly controlled. In essence, you tell people, "Do the job right and on time and you can be your own boss." For example, getting rid of time clocks and rigid working hours could be a freedom reward. Or you might supply people with ways to measure their own output and quality and tell them you don't care how the job gets done as long as they get the right results. Or you might permit people to do part of their work at home or away from the job site if the nature of the work permits it. Like time off, freedom is a very powerful incentive for younger workers. As one worker put it, "I don't mind being pushed as long as I can steer."

Reward #8: Personal Growth

Like advancement, this is a crucial reward for professional and technical people. For example, computer specialists can command excellent salaries, working conditions and fringe benefits almost anywhere. The way to keep them loyal and performing is to give them interesting work, coupled with an opportunity to learn new skills and grow in their chosen field. While advancement is very important to managers, technical specialists emphasize personal growth and fulfillment in their work.

Personal-growth rewards can be given in two basic ways. First, give people new tasks that challenge their creative ability and provide them with the chance to prove themselves and grow. Second, reward top performers with training and educational opportunities. For example, attendance at a seminar, enrollment in a course or a trip to another part of the country to study a new process could all be used as personal-growth incentives.

Reward #9: Fun

In some jobs, no matter what you do, it is difficult to get people interested or to make the work enjoyable. But very often people will get out of sick beds or come to work in a blizzard just because it's so much fun to be there. A good manager consciously builds fun into the workplace and uses it as an incentive. In essence, you tell people, "As long as we reach our goals, we can have fun too."

Since fun is different things to different people, ask your group how it would like to make the workplace more enjoyable. Many companies have sports and health facilities on the premises, but fun doesn't have to be that elaborate or expensive. How about a bulletin board for jokes, stories and candid photographs? Or parties, complete with refreshments, to celebrate birthdays, marriages, births, promotions, etc.? Or a big bash for achieving major goals? Would piped-in music help?

No matter what incentives you use to make work fun, there is one rule that almost always makes work productive and fun:

MAKE PEOPLE FEEL LIKE WINNERS.

Be sure that everyone has important, achievable goals and feels like part of a very special, winning team. People love to identify with success and they will do almost anything for the privilege.

Reward #10: Prizes

The way to reward performance with prizes, like rewarding with recognition, is limited only by imagination. Family dinners paid by the company, sports or theater tickets, vacation trips, gift certificates, trading stamps, company products or services, and appliances are all common examples of prize incentives.

A St. Louis hardware company used prizes to solve its absenteeism and tardiness problems. Workers who came to work on time for a month were eligible to participate in a drawing with one prize awarded for every twenty-five eligible workers. And workers with six months' perfect attendance were eligible to draw for a television set. Both tardiness and absenteeism rates plummeted, and sick-leave costs dropped 62 percent.

In summary, depending on the person, the job and the situation, all ten rewards can be very effective ways to get good performance. How to go about choosing rewards is covered in Action Plan 2. But for now, keep this one key point in mind:

MONEY AND RECOGNITION ARE
THE TWO MOST POWERFUL REWARDS.

You have learned ten different ways to reward good work and ten types of behavior to reward. Put them together to expand the chart on page 90 and you get the 10/10 Management System: ten different ways to reward ten important kinds of behavior:

USE THESE 10 REWARDS	TO REWARD	INSTEAD OF
1. Money	1. Solid solutions	1. Quick fixes
2. Recognition	2. Risk taking	2. Risk avoiding
3. Time off	3. Applied creativity	3. Mindless conformity
4. A piece of the action	4. Decisive action	4. Paralysis by analysis
5. Favorite work	5. Smart work	5. Busywork
6. Advancement	6. Simplification	6. Needless complication
7. Freedom	7. Quietly effective behavior	7. Squeaking joints
8. Personal growth	8. Quality work	8. Fast work
9. Fun	9. Loyalty	9. Turnover
10. Prizes	10. Working together	10. Working against

You won't be able to reward all ten kinds of good behavior equally nor should you even try. Your job is to decide which kinds of behavior are most important in a given area or job and provide the greatest rewards for that behavior. To help you decide what is most important use these guidelines:

1. Reward solid solutions to ensure the achievement of long-range goals.
2. Reward risk taking, applied creativity, and decisive action to boost the spirit of entrepreneurship.
3. Reward smart work, simplification, quietly effective behavior and quality work to improve productivity.
4. Reward loyalty and working together to foster teamwork and cooperation.

In the final analysis, management is and always will be much more of an art than a science, and your success depends as much on your judgment and skill as any other factor. I can only supply you with canvas, brush, easel, palette of colors and a few lessons. Producing the masterpiece is up to you.

How to Be a 10/10 Manager

*The problem is to learn how to define the end results we want
. . . and create the incentives to achieve them.*

— JOHN DIEBOLD

Al, Pete and Mary all work for the same company. Al is an assistant plant manager who hasn't had a promotion in years. Al isn't incompetent. He is just bored with his job. But his office is filled with trophies won at amateur golf tournaments and his prize possession is an autographed picture of himself and Jack Nicklaus that hangs on his wall. If you drop in to see Al, chances are that you will find him practicing his putting on the office rug.

Pete works on the assembly line and hates every minute of it. Try to talk to him at work and he answers in mumbled monotones—that is, until you bring up the subject of bowling. Then his eyes light up like he runs on batteries, and he talks your ear off about the upcoming tournament he's entering.

Mary is a secretary who works at two speeds: slow and stop. Ask her to type a letter and she gives you a tortured look reminiscent of the Spanish Inquisition. Mary has been working in the same office for almost twenty-five years, and the younger workers refer to her as "the resident vegetable." But if you want to excite Mary, ask about her flowers. Her backyard is filled with lilies and her living room with ribbons won at flower shows.

In today's work world, few drop dead from exhaustion but

many quietly curl up and die from undersatisfaction. Have you ever wondered why people like Al, Pete and Mary play with such intensity but sleepwalk through their jobs? *They are not lazy.* It's because their play is giving them something they aren't getting from work. Imagine how productive they would be if they got the same kick from doing their jobs that they get from their hobbies. It is possible. Here's how you do it.

To get people excited about a hobby, career, job or any activity, the activity usually must have four key ingredients:

1. A meaningful goal.
2. A way to keep score, so people can see and measure their progress.
3. Control over achieving the goal.
4. Meaningful rewards.

Take Al's case, for example. To Al, the goal of playing winning golf has significant meaning. He keeps score by counting trophies and tallying his strokes on every hole. Although he may blame the wind, the course or the weather, Al himself has the most control over where the ball goes every time he hits it. Finally, Al finds the trophies, recognition, friendships, fresh air, scenery and self-satisfaction to be meaningful rewards for his efforts. If any one of those four factors is eliminated, Al will start to lose interest in golf. And it's a safe bet that Al's job is missing at least one of those four ingredients.

The action plan you are about to learn uses all four ingredients to keep people excited, happy and productive. Before beginning, however, let's lay the ground rules with a few key points about leading people with GMP.

• Nobody works for you. Everybody works for themselves.

• Your employees don't care about what you want one-tenth as much as they care about what they want.

• Your job is to create a reward system through which your employees get what they want, you get what you want and the right things get done.

• No reward system works if people lack the ability, the authority, the training or the tools to do the job.

• People who feel good about themselves don't automatically produce good results. But producing good results helps people to feel better about themselves. One key to happiness is doing things we do well. So don't worry about getting good attitudes. Get the right results, give the right rewards and the attitudes will take care of themselves.

• Use punishment and negative sanctions only when nothing else works and they are absolutely necessary. A positive reward system is a solid solution for shaping long-term behavior. Punishment is, at best, a quick fix and can have devastating long-term consequences.

Now that you know the key points, it is time to begin. Look at Figure 1, the Goals/Rewards Contract, on the next page. This is the basic document you will be working with.

Step 1: Choose the Results You Want

Good management always starts with solid, specific, *written* goals. Sit down with each person (or group if it's a group goal) and decide, in no uncertain terms, what key results he is to achieve by a certain date. To help people set good goals, follow these guidelines:

• Their goals should help you achieve your goals and should contribute to the achievement of company goals. Show them your goals, the company's goals, and ask, "How can you help?"

• Be sure their goals are stated in terms of results to be achieved, not activities to be performed. For example, making more phone calls is an activity. Increasing sales revenue by 20 percent in the next six months is a result.

• State goals briefly and write them down. This helps increase clarity and commitment.

• When you can, let people set their own goals. Self-set goals are more meaningful. But if people want you to set goals for them, do it. What matters most is that you both understand what has to be done.

• Set only a few goals for each person or group and rank

Figure 1.
GOALS/REWARDS CONTRACT

10/10 GOALS/REWARDS AGREEMENT

I   *name of person(s)*   agree to work toward achieving the following results by *target date* :

(In this section write the goal, including how it's measured and the agreed level of achievement.)

To make this project a winner, we must emphasize *(choose one or more and rank in order of importance)*:

____	Solid solution	____	Simplicity
____	Risk taking	____	Quiet heroics
____	Innovation	____	Quality
____	Action	____	Loyalty
____	Smart work	____	Teamwork

My (our) reward(s) for successfully achieving this goal will be:

(If the reward varies with the level of achievement, put the formula for determining rewards here.)

Agreed on   *date*   by

                                          signature of achiever

                                          signature of manager

---

them in order of importance. More than two or three goals end up becoming no goals.

• Check goals for compatibility, so that the achievement of one does not preclude achieving another.

• Goals that are challenging but attainable get the best performance. Encourage people to choose battles big enough to matter but small enough to win.

One of the most crucial things to remember about goals is this:

PEOPLE DO WHAT GETS MEASURED.

This makes it imperative that every major goal have a scoring system that reflects the results you are trying to get. Just as every golf course has a par value, every major goal should have a measurable standard of excellence.

Don't fall for the classic line "You can't measure what I do." If the performance of a person or group can't be measured, chances are that they aren't contributing much.

In deciding how to measure, keep these points in mind:

• Keep the system simple. Use only one or two measures for each goal. Otherwise, people will spend too much time measuring and too little doing.

• Measure outputs instead of activities. Performance measures should indicate progress toward results achieved. For example, here are some common performance measures for different departments:

DEPARTMENT	OUTPUT MEASURE
Sales	Dollars of sales
Accounts Payable	Number of vouchers processed
Materials	Number of line items received
Maintenance	Number of work orders completed
Custodial	Number of square feet cleaned
Design	Number of blueprints turned over to production
Production Planning	Number of lines scheduled

• The best measures give people frequent feedback so they can monitor their performance and adjust as needed.
• It's much more important to measure group goals than to measure individual goals. Team performance counts most.

When goals and measures have been decided, fill out the first part of the Goals/Rewards Contract. When filled out properly, it contains the name of the person or group, the deadline for achievement, how you are keeping score and the minimum acceptable score. For example:

I *John Davis* agree to work toward achieving the following results by *June 30, 1986*.
Increase the total dollar value of sales in my territory by at least 20 percent.

Step 2: Identify the Behavior Needed

It is important for people to know and understand their goals. But they cannot *do* a goal. They have to behave in ways that will lead to the achievement of a goal. So the next step is to identify the kinds of behavior most crucial to achieving a given goal. To identify the necessary behaviors, try this:

1. Review the goal.
2. Review the ten types of desirable behavior discussed in Part II and listed in the Goals/Rewards Contract.
3. Choose from the list kinds of behavior you feel are most crucial to achieving the goal. Rank them in order of importance and write them down.
4. Ask those responsible for achieving the goal to do the same thing without having seen your choices.
5. Meet and reach a joint agreement on what kinds of behavior are most important for successfully achieving this goal.
6. On the Goals/Rewards Contract, write a priority number next to the most important behaviors. If, for example, the most important behaviors are innovation and

teamwork, put a 1 next to innovation and a 2 next to teamwork. You will use this information in Step 4.

Step 3: Decide on the Proper Rewards

As you read this, you may be thinking to yourself, "Ho-hum. Set goals. Write them down. I've tried it before and it doesn't work. It's just a waste of time, paper and money."

The reason so many goal-setting programs fail is that the goals are not directly linked to specific rewards. Good goals only start people moving in the right direction. You need specific rewards to keep them moving. Trying to get results without rewards is like trying to run an engine without fuel. The whole premise of GMP is that the right rewards for the right behavior get the right results.

With so many ways to reward people, you may ask, "How do I decide how to reward each person?" The answer is simple: Ask them. Everyone will attach different value to a given reward. So when you sit down to set goals, take extra time to set specific rewards. Make a list of possible rewards and let people choose one or combine several. But be sure the rewards are specifically spelled out and are proportional to the importance of the goal. For group goals, be sure that each individual knows how he will be rewarded when the group achieves the goal.

Once rewards have been decided, the final part of the Goals/Rewards Contract can be filled out. If the reward is one that varies with the level of achievement, write the formula for determining rewards on the form. For example:

The reward for successfully achieving this goal will be:

Ten percent of total dollar gross sales up to $2,000,000 and 15 percent of all gross sales over $2,000,000.

Once the form is completed, it should be dated and signed by all parties to the agreement, and each person should be given a copy. Encourage people to look at their Goals/Rewards Contract at the beginning of each workday and to use it as a basis for planning daily activities.

Step 4: Use the Power of Positive Feedback

Assume you have done everything discussed so far—set goals, identified the important behaviors to achieve the goals, and chosen rewards. All you have to do now is sit back and reward people as they achieve their goals, right? Not quite. There is one more crucial piece to the puzzle—positive feedback.

Achieving a major goal can take weeks, months or even years, and people need frequent reinforcement to keep them excited and encouraged. The way to keep people enthusiastic and on target is with positive feedback. Look for the good in people and let them know you value them. Make a special effort to recognize and praise good behavior and you'll soon see that good behavior getting repeated. As Robert McNamara put it, "Brains, like hearts, go where they are appreciated."

In Step 2 you identified the most important kinds of behavior necessary to achieve a major goal. The reason for doing so was to give yourself a plan for knowing what kinds of behavior to reward with positive feedback. With that information in writing, the Goals/Rewards Contract is a complete plan for leading others with GMP. It tells you the results you want, how to measure them, how to reward them and what behavior to reinforce to get results.

In order for positive feedback to work, your message should follow these guidelines:

- Be specific.
- Be sincere. Glad-handing and superficial flattery won't work. People know when they are being conned.
- Deliver it on the spot as soon as you see the good behavior.
- Personalize it for the individual.
- Make it proportional to the importance of the behavior.
- Be concrete. When you see good behavior don't say "great job" or "keep up the good work" but rather word your message like this: "Claire, how do you do it? This is the third key contract you have landed this month. It's people like you that make all of us look good and I want

you to know how much we all appreciate and need you. It's so nice to have such a good performer and a great person to work with."

There is one more guideline to remember about giving positive feedback. Do it inconsistently. That's right, *inconsistently*. Behavior that is randomly reinforced is more likely to become habitual. For example, if Claire was praised by the boss every time she brought in a new contract, the feedback would soon be taken for granted and lose its impact. But praising good behavior on random occasions increases the odds that Claire will keep trying to get those good strokes. It's much like gambling. She knows the payoff is going to come but doesn't know when. So she keeps on trying.

When you get the right results the final step is obvious.

Step 5: Dispense Rewards, Enjoy Success and Set New Goals

This is the easy, fun part of the job. But, unfortunately, you won't always get the right results. In that case, your task is to sit down with the achiever(s) and try to decide what went wrong and how to fix it. Are the goals correct and meaningful? Did everyone responsible understand them? Did you choose the right kinds of behavior to reinforce? Are the rewards appropriate and meaningful? Did you give frequent positive feedback? Did outside forces make achieving the goal impossible? If so, what were they? What has to be changed to make success possible? Focus on problem solving and don't place the blame or allow anyone else to do so. Tell your staff their efforts are appreciated and point out the things they did well. Then get down to the business of finding out what went wrong, fix it, and try again.

Putting It All Together

The key points and guidelines for the 10/10 Management System are summarized for you in Figure 2, the 10/10 Manager's Action Plan. Keep it handy for reference as you make the transition from your current managing style to managing with

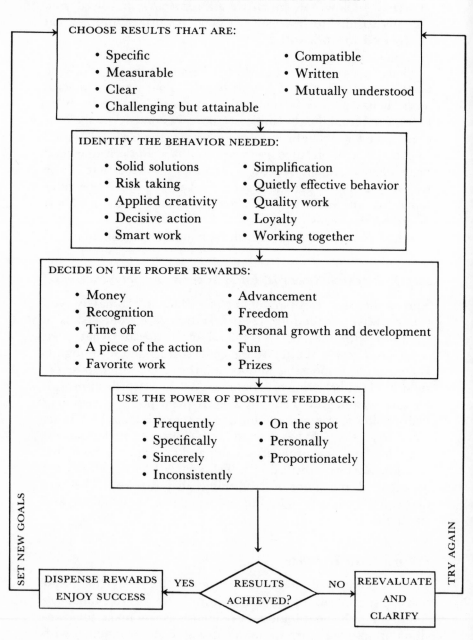

Figure 2.
THE 10/10 MANAGER'S ACTION PLAN

CHOOSE RESULTS THAT ARE:

- Specific
- Measurable
- Clear
- Challenging but attainable
- Compatible
- Written
- Mutually understood

IDENTIFY THE BEHAVIOR NEEDED:

- Solid solutions
- Risk taking
- Applied creativity
- Decisive action
- Smart work
- Simplification
- Quietly effective behavior
- Quality work
- Loyalty
- Working together

DECIDE ON THE PROPER REWARDS:

- Money
- Recognition
- Time off
- A piece of the action
- Favorite work
- Advancement
- Freedom
- Personal growth and development
- Fun
- Prizes

USE THE POWER OF POSITIVE FEEDBACK:

- Frequently
- Specifically
- Sincerely
- Inconsistently
- On the spot
- Personally
- Proportionately

SET NEW GOALS

DISPENSE REWARDS
ENJOY SUCCESS

YES ← RESULTS ACHIEVED? → NO

REEVALUATE
AND
CLARIFY

TRY AGAIN

GMP. You may also find it useful to give copies to everyone involved in the goal-setting process for handy referral.

In summary, the main point to remember about managing people with GMP is this:

YOU AREN'T MANAGING PEOPLE.
YOU'RE LEADING THEM.

Once you set up a positive reward system for achieving the right goals, people quickly become their own best managers. And that means more time and freedom for you—a pretty good reward in itself.

Managing Your Boss with GMP

> *You don't have to like and admire your boss, nor do you have to hate him. You do have to manage him, however, so that he becomes your resource for achievement, accomplishment, and . . . personal success as well.*
>
> —PETER DRUCKER

One of the most intriguing things about GMP is that anybody can use it to manage anybody. In fact, in order to manage others with rewards you must be willing to be managed. To illustrate this point, here is a personal, nonbusiness example.

I have a cat named Junior. One evening when he was about nine months old I was home alone, nursing a bad cold. I was sitting in bed reading when Junior walked into the room and crouched down like he was about to pounce on something. Suddenly he leaped into the air, hit the light switch with his paw, and the room went dark! You can imagine my state of total disbelief. I sat there thinking to myself, "Either that cat just turned out the lights or I'm tripping out on aspirin."

I got up, turned the lights back on and thought, "No one will ever believe me if I tell them about this. So I won't."

About three weeks later Junior turned out the lights again! Then I knew he could be trained to turn out the lights on command. All I had to do was start rewarding him for it. So I started putting little pieces of solid, moist cat treats on the light switch, and Junior would jump up to get the food and hit the switch. He quickly learned to associate the light switch with food. Now when I want him to perform, I get out the food, point to the light switch, and Junior does a slam-dunk that would make Julius Erving proud. My friends are totally amazed at how well I have that cat trained.

But that's only half the story. Guess what Junior does when he's in the mood for a snack? That's right, he turns out the lights. And what do you think I do? Right again, I stop what I'm doing, get the food and feed him because I want him to continue performing. On numerous occasions he has strolled into the room when I was reading, writing or rummaging through the closet and left me in a state of total darkness. But I always repress my urge to scream at him and instead get out the food and reward him. Now I ask you, who's managing whom?

Your boss is one of the most important people you can influence through rewards, and this action plan shows you how. Managing your boss is not only possible, it is essential.

In today's work world, nobody makes it completely on their own. Managing up is just as important as managing down. But many people don't realize this. Instead, they waste time complaining about the boss and assume that they are powerless to change and improve the relationship. If that sounds like you, consider this:

YOU OWN 50 PERCENT OF YOUR RELATIONSHIP WITH YOUR BOSS AND ARE 100 PERCENT IN CONTROL OF YOUR OWN BEHAVIOR. AND THE WAY YOU BEHAVE TOWARD YOUR BOSS TEACHES HIM HOW TO TREAT YOU.

For example, if you treat your boss like an omnipotent parent, you can expect him to treat you like a small child. Or the more you expect your boss to solve your problems, the less freedom you can expect him to grant you. In short, behaving like a responsible adult is the surest road to being treated like one.

The purpose of managing your boss with GMP is to make work more enjoyable and productive for both of you. It doesn't mean being an apple polisher or resorting to treacherous tactics. It's a sincere, up-front plan for improving the working relationship with the one you report to, based on the premise that you and your boss are two adults with a strong mutual interest in seeing to it that you both succeed.

Step 1: Inventory Strengths and Weaknesses

You and the boss have a lot in common. You both have a job to do and depend on each other to get it done. You both have personal goals, needs and aspirations. You both have personal strengths and weaknesses that can make or break the relationship. And you're both fallible human beings who are not likely to change very much. So the first step in managing your boss is to take stock of the two personalities and the two jobs involved. Before you can improve a working relationship you have to know the strong points, pressure points and blind spots.

Begin by gathering as much *objective* information about your boss and his job as you can. Note that I stress "objective." Understanding your boss means seeing him as he is, not as you want or expect him to be. Of course, total objectivity isn't possible, but the closer you can approximate it, the better your chances for improving the relationship. In short, you need to empathize.

You will learn a lot about your boss by writing short answers to these questions (dictating them into a tape recorder, if you prefer):

- What are your boss's major goals?
- How do you help him achieve them?
- What is he rewarded for?
- What is his boss like?
- Does he tend to share or conceal information?
- What kinds of job pressures is he under?
- Who are his allies and enemies?
- What do you like best about him?
- What do you like least?
- How could he help you be more productive?
- How could he make your work more satisfying?
- Does he like to delegate responsibility or does he keep a finger in every pie?

• Does he like things in writing or does he prefer face-to-face dialogues?

• Does he like conflict or does he prefer to manage by consensus?

  • At what time of day is he at his best?

  • What things does he do best?

  • What part of his job needs the most improvement?

  • What does he hate to do?

  • How well does he handle stress?

• Does he like to deal with one thing at a time or randomly jump from task to task?

• Is he better working with the big picture or with details?

  • How old is he?

  • What is his educational and work experience?

  • What is his family life like?

• Does he have any problems off the job that you are aware of?

  • What are his hobbies and outside interests?

  • Does he tend to be trusting or suspicious?

  • What kind of environment did he grow up in?

  • Does he have any special quirks or idiosyncrasies?

You probably won't know the answers to some of the questions. If not, don't pry. Just keep your eyes and ears open and try to find out as much about the boss as you can.

The next task is even more challenging because it requires being honest and objective about yourself. As you answer the following questions you may find it helpful to get assistance from a friend or colleague whom you trust:

  • What do you want from your job?

  • What are your job's major goals?

  • How does your boss help you achieve them?

• What conflicts and deadlines are you under pressure from?

  • What part of your job do you do best?

  • Where is your job performance weakest?

  • Do you tend to share or to conceal information?

  • What part of the job do you like most?

- What part of the job do you like least?
- Are you a morning or an afternoon person?
- Do you enjoy conflict and confrontation or do you shy away from it?
- Do you prefer communication in writing or face to face?
- How do you differ from your boss in age, education and job experience?
- How does your childhood and family background differ from your boss's?
- Do you like to work on one project at a time or do you prefer to have many irons in the fire at once?
- Are you better with details or with handling the big picture?
- How does your off-the-job life differ from that of your boss?
- Do you require close supervision or do you prefer to work alone?
- Are you a self-starter or do you need someone to get you going?
- Do you need frequent feedback or is a periodic review enough?
- Do you have any special quirks or personality traits that others may find difficult to understand?
- How do your off-the-job interests differ from your boss's?
- What kinds of jobs do you tend to put off?

After answering the questions about your boss and yourself, look them over (or listen to them) and write the answers to these questions:

1. What are your boss's three greatest strengths?
2. What are his three greatest weaknesses?
3. What are your three greatest strengths?
4. What are your three greatest weaknesses?
5. What things do you work together on most effectively?
6. What are your greatest areas of conflict and disagreement?

7. What do you feel is the greatest weakness in your relationship with your boss?

Step 2: Build on the Strengths

A good relationship with your boss (or anyone else) is achieved by building on the best that you both have to offer and making adjustments to accommodate weaknesses. As I pointed out earlier, neither you nor your boss is likely to change dramatically. You have to make the most of what you both bring to the relationship.

One of the best strength-building tactics you can use is this:

**FIND A TASK WHERE YOUR BOSS'S PERFORMANCE IS WEAK AND YOURS IS STRONG.
THEN VOLUNTEER YOUR HELP.**

For example, Evelyn's boss, Jill, was a great motivator and organizer but she had problems dealing with banks. Her loan requests for capital improvements were frequently rejected. So Evelyn took the time to survey several bankers and learned what kind of information a good loan request should contain. She then volunteered to rewrite an important loan prospectus for Jill and submit it to the bank. The loan was immediately approved and Evelyn's value soared in Jill's eyes.

Is your boss a poor writer? If you are a good writer, volunteer to ghostwrite. Does your boss hate public speaking? Volunteer to fill in and speak at public functions. The more ways you can find to complement your boss, the more he will value you. In fact, a smart boss looks for people whose strengths complement his weaknesses.

As you discover other weaknesses, take steps to accommodate them. For example, if either of you tends to be forgetful, follow up important face-to-face communications with a memo. If your boss likes to be involved in all decisions, keep him informed. If either of you is not at your best in the morning, confer about important things later in the day. If you need something from the boss, such as more feedback or help in an area you are weak in, ask for it. The key is to learn to capitalize on your respective strengths and to accommodate differences and weaknesses.

Step 3: Decide How You Want to Change Your Boss's Behavior

Your boss may be the greatest person in the world, but I bet there's something about his behavior that you would like to improve. Does he tend to be abrasive at times? Does he pull you off one job to tackle another? Does he hover over you when you need to work alone? Does he fail to give you enough feedback?

Fill in this statement: *I want my boss to . . .*

Answer it in positive terms. Don't write what you don't want. Write what you do want in specific, behavioral terms. For example:

- I want my boss to *speak more tactfully.*
- I want my boss to *give me more freedom to work on my own.*
- I want my boss to *give me more concrete information about how I'm doing.*
- I want my boss to *let me finish what I start.*

Don't make a laundry list of things about the boss you want to change. Choose only one important aspect of his behavior that needs modifying. Once you have decided this, you're ready to swing into action with GMP.

Step 4: Reward Your Boss For Any Signs of Positive Change

The key here is to reward your boss for any small resemblance of the kind of behavior you want. In short, catch him doing something good and reward him for it. Chances are that this behavior will be repeated. Then try to create situations in which he can behave even more like you want and reward him for that. Psychologists call this technique "shaping." It takes lots of patience and persistence, but it's very effective.

For example, Beverly's boss, Mark, was forever interrupting her to check up on the work he assigned. It bugged her so much that she even thought about quitting. But one day she was given a short assignment and completed it without interruption. As she turned in the job, Mark was wrestling with a quarterly report. Seizing the opportunity, Beverly said, "You know, if I could have about four uninterrupted hours, I could do the report for you. Why don't you take in a round of golf Friday afternoon and I'll wind up the report?" Mark hated to write, loved golf, and immediately agreed. (Reward #1.)

The following week Beverly told Mark's boss, in front of Mark, "I really appreciate the implicit trust Mark has in me. He gives me assignments and the freedom to show what I can do. That's important to me. But he's always available if I need his help. I like to work on my own and that's why I enjoy working for Mark." (Reward #2.) As you can see, Beverly was well on her way to shaping Mark's behavior by asking him for what she wanted and rewarding him for giving it to her.

How can you reward your boss? Here are several ideas:

• Specifically praise the good points of his behavior. Bosses need positive strokes too, but many don't get it. As one CEO remarked, "I'm not sure if people are following me or chasing me." Use the same principles for positive feedback listed in Action Plan 2 and hand out the good strokes for good behavior.

• Voice public and private support for his goals.

• Simplify his work by keeping him organized.

• Volunteer to take on routine jobs so he can have an afternoon off or more time to focus on more important tasks.

• Keep alert for ideas that will save time or money or improve the workplace and pass them along.

• Offer to serve as a sounding board for his ideas or volunteer to help him solve problems.

• Help him break in new employees by showing them the ropes and training them.

• *Tactfully* volunteer to help him with tasks for which your abilities are stronger.

• Let him and others know that you feel proud and fortunate to have the opportunity to work for him.

You can't give your boss a promotion, a bonus or a piece of the business, but you can give him a lot. How you go about doing it will play a large role in your and his success.

You may not always get the behavior you want. When that happens, just keep cool and ignore it. Instead, focus on asking and looking for positive behavior. Be ready with an assortment of ways to reward the boss when you get good behavior.

In summary, your career success depends heavily on how well you manage the one you report to. Successful boss management means building on the strengths you both bring to the relationship and working to eliminate or compensate for weaknesses. And if you want to change your boss's behavior, reward him in a way that's mutually beneficial. As in any other relationship, the surest way to get what you want is to help him get what he wants.

Be Your Own Best Timesaver

He who gains a victory over other men is strong; but he who gains a victory over himself is all powerful.

—LAO-TSE

Would you like more time and freedom to do what you want? Who wouldn't? Well, you can have it. Most of us waste about half our time. And most wasted time is due to poor habits and a lack of self-discipline on our part.

How do you acquire good habits and self-discipline? It's simple. You reward yourself for doing the right things until doing those things comes naturally. Good time management is first-rate habits made second nature.

Managing time is really a matter of managing your own behavior. And you change behavior by creating a reward system that rewards productive behavior and discourages time wasting. It's like being your own animal trainer.

This action plan won't teach you how to roll over and play dead, but it will give you plenty of ideas for getting more done in less time. It teaches you a positive and enjoyable way to motivate yourself to tackle tough projects, minimize interruptions, conquer procrastination and develop the first-rate habits, discipline and organization that will give you the winner's edge. "Until you can manage yourself you can't manage anything else" is an old but true axiom.

Before beginning, however, be sure you have a set of clear, written goals and have ranked them in order of importance.

Unless you know what results you are trying to achieve, any efforts at managing yourself will be futile. If you haven't written down your goals, do it before going any farther, following the guidelines in Action Plan 2.

Step 1: Take a Time Inventory

Remember the first time you heard or saw yourself on tape? Your likely reaction was "Oh my God! Is that me? Do I sound (or look) like that? Do I do that?" Well, take a one-week time inventory and I guarantee you will be equally surprised.

We spend most of our time in automatic, recurring patterns of behavior (habits). Some save us a lot of time and others waste time. But we are not aware of most habits until we make a conscious effort to discover them. That's why this first step is so important.

If this is your first time inventory, expect to find a lot of surprises (and not all of them will be pleasant). But taking a hard, objective look at your own behavior is one of the best favors you can do for yourself. You can't replace bad habits with good ones until you know what the bad ones are.

The way to find out where your time goes is to write down everything you do for one week. Begin by constructing a daily time-log form such as the one in Figure 3 and make a copy for each day of the week. To get the most from your time inventory, follow these instructions:

☐ 1. At the start of each day enter your name, the day and the date at the top of a time-log form. Take it with you wherever you go.

☐ 2. When you begin an activity, write down the starting time and the nature of the activity in the first two columns. Be sure to list every activity and why it occurred.

☐ 3. Rate each activity for importance and urgency using the key under Figure 3 on page 127.

For example, if you are working on an activity that is very important and very urgent, write Al in the Importance/Urgency column. Or, if it is a medium-priority, nonurgent task, write B3 in the Importance/Urgency column.

☐ 4. If the activity is a planned one, put a P in the Planned/

Figure 3.

DAILY TIME LOG					
Name ——————— Day ——————— Date ———————					
Starting Time	Activity	Imp./ Urg.	Plan./ Int.	Time Used	Comments

Importance	*Urgency*
A. Top priority (must do)	1. Must be done now
B. Medium priority (should do)	2. Should be done soon
C. Low priority	3. Not urgent

Interruption column. If it's an interruption, write an I in the Planned/Interruption column.

☐ 5. When you finish working on one activity (or are interrupted by another), write down the amount of time used in the appropriate column. Any comments or thoughts you may have about the activity—was it a waste of time? can you delegate it to someone else? do you have an idea for doing it better or faster?—write down in the comments column. These ideas will be very useful when you take stock of the week's activities.

☐ 6. At the end of the week, take inventory. Review your time-log sheets, noting the kinds of activities that occur most frequently, such as telephone calls, seeing customers, doing paperwork, visiting with colleagues, attending meetings, socializing and corresponding. Then summarize the week by constructing a time-inventory statement such as the one in Figure 4. Write down each major category of time use (including a miscellaneous category), how much time it consumed and the percentage of total time it consumed. Now you know where your time is going. Chances are that it isn't going where you thought it was. But don't get discouraged. The best of us waste two hours a day.

☐ 7. Now take several sheets of paper, your written goals and your time-inventory statement. Find a quiet spot where you can think without being interrupted. Be very honest with yourself, and after careful consideration write the answers to these questions:

- What are my three greatest time wasters?
- How much time is consumed by interruptions? Who or what is most responsible for them? How can they be reduced?
- Am I doing tasks that are urgent and unimportant? How can they be reduced or eliminated?
- What are my most and least productive times of the day?
- Whom do I need to see more of? Whom do I need to see less of?
- What activities need more time?
- What activities need less time?
- What can be eliminated or delegated?

Figure 4.

```
┌─────────────────────────────────────────────────────────────────┐
│                                                                   │
│                   TIME-INVENTORY STATEMENT                        │
│                                                                   │
│                                                                   │
│      Name _____        Week of _____        │
│                                                                   │
│                                                 Percentage of     │
│      Major Activities        Time Consumed       Total Time       │
│                                                                   │
│                                                                   │
│                                                                   │
│                                                                   │
│                                                                   │
└─────────────────────────────────────────────────────────────────┘
```

- Am I trying to do too much?
- Am I procrastinating?
- What habits or tendencies are causing me to waste time?

When you have finished making your time-inventory statement and answering the questions, go out and treat yourself to a nice reward. Buy yourself that new shirt or handbag you've been admiring. Or have dinner at that new restaurant you've been wanting to try. Give yourself a pat on the back for having the courage to discover your own weaknesses. It's a tough exercise but one that will pay big dividends if you follow through on the remaining steps. Remember, a fault recognized is half-corrected.

Step 2: Choose a New Habit

Have you ever read a book or been to a seminar on time management? If so, you know they give you literally hundreds of ways to work smarter. But most of them don't tell you how to go about making all those good techniques become as natural as brushing your teeth. The answer is simple:

CHOOSE ONLY ONE NEW TECHNIQUE AT A TIME AND PRACTICE IT FOR THREE WEEKS.

It takes about three weeks to transform a new way of behaving into a comfortable habit. But most people fail to realize this. Instead, they try to make radical, wholesale changes in their behavior, find it unbearable and go back to their old, comfortable habits. This is the case with people who go on crash diets, find them intolerable and ultimately end up gaining more weight than they lost. The key to making lasting changes in your behavior is to make them gradually, smoothly and systematically.

Review your time-inventory questions. Now choose *one* new habit that you feel will have the greatest time-saving value and resolve to practice it for three weeks without fail. For example, here are what I call the troublesome twelve, one dozen of the most commonly reported time wasters at work. Each is accompanied by a new habit to replace the old one.

Once you decide on a new habit, announce the change to others and start practicing it immediately. Don't wait until you feel like changing or you'll wait forever. Just act the way you want to be and soon you'll be the way you act. It is much easier to act yourself into feeling than to feel yourself into acting.

TIME WASTER	NEW HABIT
1. Lack of planning	1. Make a daily to-do list and rank items in order of importance. Then schedule your day to work on the most important tasks during prime time, the time when your energy level is highest. That way, you give your best self to the most important jobs.
2. Paper shuffling	2. Resolve to handle each piece of paper only once. Every time you pick up a piece of paper, throw it away, file it or do something to move it on its way.

3. Cluttered desk

   3. Clear the top of your desk and put out of sight everything except the item you're currently working on.

4. Routine and trivia

   4. Save trivial items and do them in batches. Hold trivia sessions during nonprime time, when your energy level is low.

5. Trying to do too much

   5. Don't do anything unnecessary or that you can give to someone else. Practice saying no politely and rapidly. Slow down. The key to doing more is to do less better.

6. Afternoon drowsiness

   6. Eat a light lunch.

7. Too many interruptions

   7. Establish quiet hours during which you can work undisturbed.

8. Drop-in visitors

   8. Have visitors screened. Establish visiting hours. Close your door. Schedule breaks and lunch hours to see those you need to see.

9. The telephone

   9. Have calls screened. Establish a telephone time for placing and receiving calls. Put a three-minute hourglass by your telephone and use it.

10. Meetings

   10. Never go to meetings if you can send someone else. Establish starting and ending times. Schedule meetings back to back, before lunch or at the end of the day.

11. Indecision

   11. Accept risks as inevitable. Gather information, give yourself a deadline and make a choice. That's what you are paid to do.

12. Procrastination

   12. Break up that overwhelming job you're putting off into as many small jobs as you can. Give yourself a deadline for completing the entire project and work on it a little bit every day starting today.

Step 3: Choose a Fitting Reward

This is the enjoyable part of the action plan. When you choose a new habit, also pick out a reward you can give yourself after three weeks of consistent success at practicing the new habit. This will be your incentive to practice the new behavior until it becomes second nature to you. The reward for your success and self-discipline need not be enormous, but it should be meaningful to you. Make it whatever you want—a movie, a piece of jewelry, a record album or tape, a new book or a weekend trip.* Just be sure to write down the new habit and the reward before you begin. And keep this in mind: Every good, new habit you acquire has the built-in rewards of more free time, less stress and higher productivity·with long-range payoffs. You are gaining the skills that turn talent into ability.

Step 4: Reward Yourself for Three Weeks of New Behavior

If you unfailingly practice a new behavior for three weeks, it will probably become a well-ingrained habit. So give yourself a reward, smile at yourself in the mirror and choose another new habit (and reward) to practice for the next three weeks. Keep repeating the self-management cycle and over a period of months you will begin to see drastic and lasting improvements in your productivity.

---

*The only thing you may not use as a reward is reverting to your old behavior. For example, if you've been eating a light lunch on workdays for three weeks, don't reward yourself with a gourmet lunch during the week. Save it for weekends or dinner.

If you catch yourself slipping into the old behavior, turn the clock back to day one and start counting over. Once you successfully practice the new habit for three straight weeks, reward yourself, enjoy your success and go back to Step 2.

You must be very honest with yourself to make this action plan work. Be sure to reward yourself for three successful weeks of practicing a new habit, and don't reward yourself until you have done it for three straight weeks. If you have trouble trusting yourself, share your plan with someone and ask him to watch you. Or better yet, give him the reward you picked out for yourself and tell him to give it to you only after you reach your goal.

As you can see, GMP is a great tool for managing your time. But it's actually much more than that. GMP enables you to take complete control of your life and become whatever you want to be. You can use the self-management cycle to help yourself diet, exercise, learn a new skill or hobby or improve any aspect of your life that involves conscious behavior. In the final analysis, *only you* can control these three things:

1. How you think.
2. How you feel.
3. How you behave.

And that's all you need to take charge of your life. Do it!

Epilogue

Now you know the greatest management principle in the world. The next time you hear an expert belaboring the complexities of an organizational problem, you don't have to stay confused—just ask the magic question and everything will come clearly into focus. Most important, practice using GMP to make life better for those you work with, your boss and yourself. Because the bottom line is simply this:

EVERYBODY WORKS SMARTER WHEN THERE'S SOMETHING IN IT FOR THEM.

Summary of
The Greatest Management Principle in the World

The Basics

1. The things that get rewarded get done.
2. If you aren't getting the results you want, ask the magic question: *"What's being rewarded?"*

Strategy: What to Reward

THE 10/10 MANAGEMENT SYSTEM

REWARD:

1. Solid solutions
2. Risk taking
3. Applied creativity
4. Decisive action
5. Smart work
6. Simplification
7. Quietly effective behavior

INSTEAD OF:

1. Quick fixes
2. Risk avoiding
3. Mindless conformity
4. Paralysis by analysis
5. Busywork
6. Needless complication
7. Squeaking joints

WITH:

1. Money
2. Recognition
3. Time off
4. A piece of the action
5. Favorite work
6. Advancement
7. Freedom

8. Quality work
9. Loyalty
10. Working together

8. Fast work
9. Turnover
10. Working against

8. Personal growth
9. Fun
10. Prizes

Action: Who and How to Reward

MANAGE OTHERS

1. Choose the results you want.

2. Identify the behavior needed.
3. Decide on the proper rewards.

4. Use the power of positive feedback.

5. Dispense rewards, enjoy success and set new goals.

MANAGE YOUR BOSS

1. Inventory strengths and weaknesses.

2. Build on the strengths.
3. Decide how you want to change your boss's behavior.

4. Reward your boss for signs of positive change.

MANAGE YOURSELF

1. Choose a new habit.

2. Choose a fitting reward.
3. Practice the habit for three straight weeks.

4. Give yourself the reward, enjoy success and choose a new habit.

The Bottom Line: Everybody works smarter when there's something in it for them.

What's Your Favorite Way to Manage With GMP?

I have presented the best ideas and experiences I know of in this program for using GMP to bring out the best in your people, your boss and yourself. But this book is only the starting point. I'd like to give you and others even more information on how to get better results with rewards.

Do you have a favorite way of using rewards to manage others, your boss and yourself? Have you discovered positive behavior that needs to be rewarded instead of negative behavior that tends to be rewarded? Have you found any effective rewards that I didn't mention? Please share your discoveries and success stories. Write and tell me the best, worst, most useful and funniest experiences you have ever witnessed that apply to GMP. Type up your thoughts and mail them to:

Michael LeBoeuf
P.O. Box 9504
Metairie, Louisiana 70005

Be sure to include your mailing address and preferably a telephone number. Should I plan to use your example in my next book, I will contact you for permission and to verify the material. Your reward will be a copy of the new book. Don't worry about confidentiality. Names and places will be changed to ensure anonymity where appropriate. However, if you want your name included in the acknowledgments as a contributor, I will be happy to list it. Thanks for sharing your experiences with rewards-based management and I'll look forward to hearing from you soon.

Best regards,
MICHAEL LEBOEUF, PH.D.

Index